SLEEPWALKING
ON A
TIGHTROPE

TRANSCEND LIFE'S CHALLENGES THROUGH LEARNING
THE LIFE BALANCE ADVANTAGE

MARK ARMIENTO

ISBN-13: 978-1511495448

Book Layout & Design by PIXEL eMarketing INC.

Legal Disclaimer

DEDICATED TO...

The oldest living angel, my mother Helen Demelia and those angels who have passed over; my great Aunt Frances, and my infant son, Gavin Marcus. My wife of over 35 years, Mary Riddle-Armiento, mother of our four sons; Gavin, Brandon, Alex and Jake - who have supported and loved me throughout my many years of soul searching.

During the thirty years that I have been writing this book, my central focus has been on answering one fundamental question: What healthy guidance could I impart to my sons regarding how to transcend life's adversity and live their lives with spiritual purpose?

My soul's desire is to grant those who desire to awaken to timeless wisdom- the priceless insight that I could only have fantasized about during my formative years.

Wishing all those who read "Sleepwalking on a Tightrope" a life-changing awakening to their spirit within.

ACKNOWLEDGMENTS

To all the many wise guides that have left their eternal mark within the words you are about to read.

To all those who have listened and displayed the exceptional courage to accept the Life Balance Advantage into their lives; from the Anthonys, Brians, Frances, Georges, Leslies, Lisas, Jaimes, Janets, Jo-Anns, Katherines, and Pattys to the Peters, Jims, Joans, Marks, Mannys, Mehdis, Phobays, Steves, Stephs, and the remarkable Shenettas and Vinnknees.

And a special note of gratitude to Jaime Boyaca for his gifted and artistic book cover design, Lorna, for her keen editing eye, and certainly to my new Canadian friend, Melissa Se.

CONTENTS

INTRODUCTION
WHEN LIFE HAPPENS AND YOUR INNER VOICE SCREAMS

We all have an inner voice that lives inside us like a constant companion. It follows us wherever we go, either enriching or polluting our lives. This inner voice is driven to ask questions—about how you feel, who you are, and what your place is in the world. This voice wants answers. If it does not get them, it can distort the way that you think.

Asking important life questions is something that every human being faces. But it is not enough to simply ask them. You actually have to seek out the answers. These answers cannot be found in the pages of a book or on a phone call with a friend. They can only be discovered within yourself.

Life then becomes a journey. Each of us must find the right questions to ask and then answer them in a way that satisfies our inner selves. You will know immediately if you have been neglecting your inner voice because it has been screaming at you. Your thoughts and internal self-questions have become dark and dreary. Somehow it seems like you have turned on yourself, but you are not sure why or how.

- Do you often wonder why bad things happen to you?
- Do you feel like you can never seem to "catch a break" no matter how hard you try?

Perhaps you have been asking the wrong questions. Maybe, just maybe, those wrong questions have been driving you to seek out the wrong kinds of answers. The adversity that we face is directly connected to this process of self-limiting thought.

You need to become aware that your inner voice has been asking disastrous questions and that aligning your entire person has been aligned with seeking out unsuccessful results. Few people are aware that our thoughts direct our actions and that these create our reality. Negative life events often happen as a result of these dark, poorly conceived questions.

So many approach me through my clinical practice with feelings of life dissatisfaction. They seek succor for their sources of anxiety and lack of self-worth—hating their bodies, anxious over their tomorrows, emotionally unresponsive, or feeling out of control. They mention intimacy complaints and challenges with discovering their true soul mate accompanied with complaints of suffering from meaninglessness and devoid of a sense of spiritual purpose in their life's journey.

What drives these chronic complaints? What fuels these older, conditioned, limited beliefs?

Weight Loss

- 68.5% of adults are overweight or obese; 34.9% are obese.
- 31.8% of children and adolescents are overweight or obese; 16.9% are obese.
- 30.4% of low-income preschoolers are overweight or obese.

Obesity is one of the leading preventable causes of death worldwide. In the United States, obesity is estimated to cause 111,909 to 365,000[1] deaths per year.

We have heard all our lives to "eat right" and "exercise," but that is a tall order in our hypocritical society, where a McDonald's lies on the same corner as your fitness center. With a world full of options, doing the right thing is not always easy and does not always make sense until it is too late.

Marriage & Dating

About 2.5 million Americans[2] get divorced each year. Marriage failure rates have gone as high as 50%. What is it about marriage that is not working for so many people? We will find out.

Money & Careers

Everyone has their own version of the American Dream. But for most people, money is an important benchmark for success. And yet so few are financially secure by the time they retire.

Economic inequality is set to reach a worrying tipping point next year, when the richest 1 percent will control more than half of the world's wealth. Do you have a roadmap to financial security?

A lot of people go to work hating their jobs and are completely unfulfilled by their careers. What is the secret to finding that dream job?

---

1   Trust for America's Health Obesity Report 2010. http://www.scribd.com/doc/35125810/Trust-for-America-s-Health-Obesity-Report-2010
2   Marriage and divorce statistics. http://www.avvo.com/legal-guides/ugc/marriage-divorce-statistics

Bad Habits

Smoking ordinary cigarettes is known to cause all kinds of health issues. Chronic use of marijuana, pain pills, and alcohol are more in style than ever before. But what about balance? Is too much of a good thing bad? Is too much of a bad thing worse?

Psychological Challenges

Panic and anxiety disorders, bipolar disorder, sleep and eating disorders, depression, ADHD, and PTSD—if you do not have one of these, there is a good chance that you know someone that does. We are living in the mental health age, and these challenges need to be explored.

Managing Stress

People are working more hours. It is getting tougher and tougher to keep up with the bills. The economy, layoffs, relationship problems, family issues—we all have a lot on our plates. Simple and effective stress management techniques are vital to life balance in the 21st century.

What if you could be more mindful about the questions that you ask? That internal voice could break free, and you would be released from negative emotions and self-limiting dialogue and learn how to live a healthier physical, mental, emotional, relational, and spiritual life. You could find the answers to the right questions and begin to manifest your positive intentions!

I have been a clinical counselor for more than thirty years. This book is for people like you that want to find real answers to these enigmatic life questions, find happiness, and discover their true selves without having to spend a fortune on therapy. Helping yourself begins with healing, and all healing begins with new knowledge.

Consider this a guide for your inner voice.

PART I

THE PRINCIPLES
OF BEING AWAKE!

CHAPTER 1
SLEEPWALKING THROUGH LIFE?

"Our worst fear is not that we are inadequate, our deepest fear is that we are powerful beyond measure. It is our light, not our darkness that most frightens us. We ask ourselves, 'Who am I to be brilliant, gorgeous, talented, and fabulous?'

Actually, who are you not to be?

You are a child of God: your playing small doesn't serve the world. There is nothing enlightened about shrinking so that other people won't feel insecure around you. We were born to manifest the glory of God within us. It is not just in some of us, it is in everyone and as we let our own light shine we unconsciously give other people permission to do the same. As we are liberated from our fear, our presence automatically liberates others."

Marianne Williamson

There are two types of connection that people have with their inner voices or selves: the conscious connection and the unconscious connection. Unfortunately, for most people, they neglect to realize that they have a rich internal life. It is one that is brimming with self-talk and the emotional reactions that come from this ongoing dialogue with yourself.

When you are not consciously aware of your inner voice, it becomes like you are sleepwalking through life. Instead of finding your way, you start crashing into everything. Life starts to become a hostile place. But this is not how you were meant to live. If you have been sleepwalking through life, then consider this your early morning wake-up call.

The Concept of Being Asleep

When your inner voice is left to its own devices, it operates on autopilot. And like any supercomputer left to build its own algorithms unattended, bugs develop. There is a direct connection between what happens in your life and how often you consider what is happening with your inner voice. The two are incontrovertibly linked!

Sleepwalkers will not understand the importance of discovering how to manifest mental, emotional, physical, relational, and spiritual balance, because they are sucked into the outside world. By living with their eyes closed, they do not realize that their silent intentions are connected to the experiences in their lives.

Without awareness or consciousness that there even is a relationship between your thoughts, feelings, and behaviors, you are doomed to unconsciously repeat old, conditioned responses that you developed as a young person. This buggy logic is the reason why so many people are unable to overcome their own thoughts or feelings about things.

A sleepwalker cannot see themselves for what they are nor can they find their way. The path for them will always be treacherous because they do not trust themselves enough to open their eyes. Ironically, if they learned how, their lives would be completely healed. Then they could walk down any path they chose, free of obstacles!

During my many years of working with families and individuals with serious problems, the common thread has always been this connection to their inner voice. Sleepwalkers need to be awakened in order to realize what they have been missing.

The universe, in all its glory, tries to wake up those of us who insist on sleepwalking. It throws life events and adversity in your path to raise your level of consciousness so that you might become aware and awaken from your deep sleep.

Defining the Opportunity

What if I told you that right now you are sleepwalking through life?

No one wants to admit it, but it is clear to see. You probably picked up this book because you knew things needed to change, and you wanted to know how to change them. You opened your eyes for just a moment and let in enough light to start you down a new path. For that...well done! Each of us has the opportunity to wake up and thrive.

The sheer diversity of religious and spiritual experience today is evidence that people have attempted to understand the universe since man began. The mystics, saints, sages, scientists, writers, and artists that have lived throughout time have all made contact with a level of consciousness that went beyond what society defined as "life."

What is the meaning of life? Or more to the point—what is the meaning of "my life"? This has always been the ultimate question. The spirit inside[3] each of us, the one that controls our inner voices, wants to be heard. I believe that our spiritual sides are grossly underrepresented in the world. Spirituality is not considered a vital human function.

Considering that our biological, psychological, and social sides are all hailed as the very "crux" of life, why are so few people happy? Maybe there is something big that is missing. What if that big thing has to do with our internal selves?

Our spiritual life occurrences happen unconsciously to us all the time. They happen, and then they are stored away deep inside our subconscious minds. This is where our automatic programming lives.

---

3   Why Is Spirituality Important?, http://www.takingcharge.csh.umn.edu/enhance-your-wellbeing/purpose/spirituality/why-spirituality-important

Our subconscious mind drinks in the world, and we chalk "who we are" or "what happens" up to coincidence or serendipity.

These spiritual experiences can manifest in the form of sudden inspiration, a feeling of being intimately connected to nature, or like we are part of a much larger whole—a cosmic plan. They happen while looking at amazing art, when hearing an incredible piece of music, or during a private moment of transcendent awareness.

When they happen, it feels as though we are being guided by a force that we cannot explain. Meaningful coincidences and synchronicities enter our lives, and we get the overwhelming feeling like something magical has happened. These mystical occurrences have a significant impact on our lives, and we should seek them out more often.

The Start of Something Big: Reality Hits

Do you ever get the feeling that something big is about to happen?

I want this to be one of those moments for you. When you realize that life is more than a collection of your physical, mental, and social experiences, then you will also realize that you have been ignoring that inner voice inside of you.

Let's not get too deep into spirituality just yet. For now, all I want you to know is that your spirit connects you to more things in your life than you realize. That inner voice that you have been hearing is part of your spirit or your true inner self. It has been struggling to get your attention and has fallen into a dire state of disrepair.

Your reality and everything in it is a direct result of how much attention you pay to your inner voice or spiritual side.[4] It acts as an alarm system for our needs, wants, and desires. It tells us when things do not feel right and helps us recover from adversity that impacts the body, mind, and our social sphere.

Human beings are not supposed to live without meaning and purpose in their lives. The irony, of course, is that everything in our

---

4   Science Proves Importance of Spirituality in Life and Health, http://lifeandself.com/why-is-spirituality-important-the-importance-of-spirituality/

society attempts to distract us from finding out what really makes us happy. It is only when we are able to really listen to ourselves that we start asking the right questions and getting the right answers.

Then we start to understand our true purpose for existing, our driving force, and the lessons that we are meant to learn in this life. Reality is different for everyone—that much is true. But when you wake up from your sleepwalk—no matter where you are in life—your inner voice can guide you to better things, places, and people.

You hear stories about these "miracle" people that come from nothing and end up with everything. These individuals discovered early that the fastest route to happiness and fulfillment is to pay attention to that inner voice. It is the connection that we all have to spirituality and the universe.

My hope is that as you read this self-help book and begin your own awakening, you start to demystify your actions and embrace these new lines of thinking. They will help you keep your eyes wide open as you walk along new paths. You will find out why this is so important as you journey through the book and heal your past experiences.

Meeting the Challenge

Once you have recognized and embraced this new opportunity, you need to see that a challenge exists alongside it.

Many of us still remain unconsciously incompetent when it comes to recognizing the spiritual experiences in our lives. As I mentioned, those that are unaware of our spiritual potential—due to lack of direct experience, supporting beliefs, or consciousness—will often see their lives as completely meaningless.

When there is an absence of spirituality,[5] there is an absence of self. The inner voice inside you becomes nothing more than a self-loathing narrative that pulls you down. When your life is devoid of meaning, you will never be able to recognize the importance of living

---

5   Kathy Juline, Creating A New Earth Together, http://www.eckharttolle.com/article/
Awakening-Your-Spiritual-Lifes-Purpose

a balanced life—where your mind, body, and spirit work in unison.

Worse yet, you will never even reach a state where you believe pursuing these goals is worth your time. If this is you, you might have a bad case of a condition I like to call "yearning for meaning," whether you want to acknowledge it or not. When you yearn for meaning in your life, your inner self acts out, rebelling against the world.

This inevitably leads to self-destructive behaviors like compulsive gambling, alcohol and drug abuse, eating and sleep disorders, financial challenges, anxiety, panic, depression, and dysfunctional relationships—all in a desperate attempt to mask the overwhelming symptoms of shunning your inner voice. The pain of an ordinary, meaningless existence is too much for anyone to take.

And it is not the truth of your life. The real tragedy is that you have become completely closed to a fundamental side of you that has been fighting to break free. Acknowledging and even reveling in your physical, mental, emotional, and social dimensions all mean nothing without the spirit there to find meaning in what you are doing.

A patient of mine might have all the material comforts in the world—a loving mate, a set of great kids, and a promising future—and still be miserable. Why? Because he or she has spent their life focusing on physical, mental, and emotional challenges and not spiritual ones. You must stop to look inside to answer those questions that the inner voice is still asking!

Meeting the challenge here means acknowledging that reality is subjective and changeable. Until you embrace your inner voice, you will always feel disquiet inside yourself and feel that undercurrent of meaninglessness and dissatisfaction with life. This is when you live to escape, to run away from those feelings. This is when destruction and disaster strike.

The Work That Must Be Done on You

"Health" is a buzzword today used to sell a lot of products to people.

Gym equipment, weight loss supplements, spa visits—there is a never-ending supply of "health" if only you have the money to buy it. Unfortunately, real health—the kind that restores you and gives you wellbeing—cannot be bought. It can only be nurtured.

The body, the mind, our emotions, our relationships, and the spirit are interconnected. They make up who and what you are. Leave one of them out, and you are not whole. Keeping that in mind—do you feel whole? Or do you feel like there has been something missing from your life for the longest time? If you feel loss, that is because your inner voice has been ignored.

Our Western society rewards individual parts of things. We love focusing on pieces of a whole instead of the whole. Just look at how many doctors there are to get a good idea. After all, parts make it easier to understand a single thing. It simplifies matters, but a lot becomes lost in the big picture. And every human being is a big picture.

You are not a healthy body and an astute mind alone. Within those rippling muscles and advanced IQ, there is a voice! It has been learning and helping you live for the longest time. It has become so good at this that your very emotions have been programmed according to the things that it has experienced throughout your life.

To truly be healthy living in life balance, you need physical, mental, emotional, relational, and spiritual wellbeing. I feel as though leaving one of these out is a critical mistake too many people make in today's fast-paced, consumer-driven society. Not everything worth getting exists on the outside. Sometimes the best things in life are inside, but they have been locked away.

Potential, for example, is one of these things. No one understands how some people can be extraordinary while others can barely learn. Perhaps some are more in touch with their potential than others? Right now you are like an unfinished sculpture.

The only way to access true wellness-life balance and real health is to turn inward and work on the hard stuff. Getting in touch with your inner voice, how you feel, how you think, and how you socialize and then actively changing it to improve your life is what you have needed all along. The conscious mind drives the subconscious one[6]— it is time you introduced them to each other.

The Balance Solution

To rectify the problem that you have been living with for all of this time, you will need to refocus your efforts on restoring life balance. You must rediscover the divine potential that was granted to you when you were born.

This means listening to your inner voice and what it has been saying. The journey involves an awakening process, where you finally become aware of those conscious and subconscious beliefs, attitudes, and behaviors that have been preventing you from manifesting this true divine potential.

In other words, you need to rediscover the meaning in your life. This awakened awareness must include an appreciation of the importance of maintaining a real balance[7] within yourself so that you can function as a whole human being. This is where you will find the stability you need to maintain your life energy.

A true balanced life will be reflected in every aspect of who you are. You will feel physically energized, mentally focused, emotionally centered, interpersonally connected, and spiritually aligned. Many people believe that each of us represents divinity in disguise, yearning to unfold and fully materialize.

When we begin to experience our lives as the miraculous unfolding of the spirit within, we begin to become aware of the true nature of our magnificent existence. This awakened divinity does not come easily. It demands long-term commitment and dedication to attaining true Life Balance in your lifetime.

---

6   Benedict Carey, Who's Minding the Mind?, http://www.nytimes.com/2007/07/31/ health/psychology/31subl.html?pagewanted=all&_r=0

7   Mary Kurus, Physical, Emotional, Mental, and Spiritual Health, http://www. mkprojects.com/fa_PEMHealth.htm

Balance is something that every religion and spiritual sect has spoken about at length. While religion is not spirituality, many religions even support the idea of balance because it is so critical to the development of human consciousness.

You have been living an unbalanced life, and it shows with everything that you do. Self-destructive behaviors, not experiencing meaning in life, and shutting out your inner voice have left you feeling miserable, unfulfilled, and angry inside. People were never meant to live this way—by embracing the material world and excluding the internal one.

Your solution is to find balance so that the energy you are gifted with is directed at the right people and places. When you are in touch with your inner voice and both your conscious and subconscious minds are connected, you achieve a new kind of super power—the ability to do whatever it is that you want to do most.

Waking Up From the Sleepwalk

Right now, there is a good chance that you are sleepwalking.

Yes, it is possible to be sleepwalking through life and not even realize it. The fact is that a very high percentage of the population does this and never recovers from it. By sleepwalking through life, they keep their potential to lead a fulfilling, happy, and balanced existence locked away from themselves until their last breath.

You do not want to be like one of these people. I strongly suggest that you take this book as a sign that you have wandered blind down the wrong paths for too long. Now it is your turn to wake up. I know, you might be very comfortable in your sleepwalk—after all, people become set in their ways. They learn to enjoy suffering and find pleasure in their misery.

But again, this is just your inner voice trying to make the best of a bad situation. It still needs your help to break free. Waking up from the sleepwalk means understanding how your two dominant minds work. There is the conscious and subconscious mind that you have to take into account.

The conscious mind is the reality you live in every day. What you are aware of right now is constructed by your conscious mind. You know that there are things happening on the outside of you and that there are things happening inside of you that you do not quite understand. For example, you continue to breathe, but you do not think about it often.

The subconscious[8] mind is where all of your accessible information is stored. You become aware of this information once you direct your attention to it. Your memory, and the feelings that you have surrounding your memories for example, are part of your subconscious mind. You know how to get back to your childhood home because you lived there.

You can chat to someone on the phone while driving and thinking about work. You can access this subconscious information whenever you choose. It is all there. Some memories need triggers to be accessed; others do not. The subconscious mind is still largely a mystery to modern-day science.

One thing is for sure: knowing how to use each mind contributes to helping you wake up and embrace your future as a whole, balanced human being.

What It Means to Be Awake!

Imagine the things you could do and feel if only you were whole!

Waking up from sleepwalking is a transcendent but difficult experience. When you finally do recognize that voice within and begin to hear what it has been saying, it might startle you at first. You might realize you are not where you should be in life.

When both of your minds are working in harmony[9] and your physical, mental, emotional, relational, and spiritual sides are

---

8   Subconscious Mind and Its Impact on Our Behaviour, http://www.tonyfahkry.com/subconscious-mind-and-its-impact-on-our-behaviour/

9   Signs and Symptoms of a Spiritual Awakening, http://in5d.com/signs-and-symptoms-of-a-spiritual-awakening/

aligned, you will finally see things clearly for the first time. Going through an intimate spiritual awakening can be harrowing, but the rewards are worth it.

- You will find that your personal intuition and "feelings" about things become heightened and you get an innate sense during life experiences. You might also begin to notice people's energy as being either positive or negative.

- A very strong desire will emerge in you as you are driven to find or create yourself once again. You might change your social group, your job, or your behavior. You may find that behaviors you once believed you could never live without simply fall away and are replaced by more meaningful things.

- You become aware of recurring patterns in your own behavior and in the people closest to you too. Relationships seem to stretch wide open as you see them for what they really are and how they have been affecting you.

- You may be overcome with a feeling that you have changed for the better and have an affinity for places where lots of people gather, such as restaurants and clubs.

- You will have a wide range of physical experiences as the body releases years of physical, emotional, karmic, and mental toxic waste. This may make you tired or thirsty or give you headaches depending on your past.

- You will feel a stronger connection with nature and will enjoy introspection more, along with boundless physical energy and a strong feeling of wellbeing.

- Creative bursts are likely to happen more often as you tap into what you really need and feel. A desire to break away from restrictions and things that make you unhappy will also become part of your development.

Being awake means being whole, being free. It means embracing all of what it means to be a human being and allowing who you truly are to guide what you want to do. When you learn this trust and unification within yourself, amazing things happen.

CHAPTER 2
AWAKEN YOUR AUTHENTIC SELF

"We must let go of the life we planned, so as to expect the one that is waiting for us."
Joseph Campbell

The most authentic version of yourself combines all of the major elements involved in being a functional human being. After all, the goal of life is to find purpose and happiness, and this cannot be achieved when you are walking around feeling unfulfilled or like part of yourself is missing all of the time.

To awaken this part of yourself is to realize that there is still so much more to learn about the human condition. Your body, mind, and spirit make a powerful trio of allies and when used harmoniously, can produce incredible results. Consider this your first adventure into the hidden self that has been with you since birth.

Adventures into the Hidden Self

We are all born with inner wisdom, and that wisdom evolves as we grow into who we are now. What many people do not realize, however, is that we are also products of our past experiences. When your inner self gets hurt, it learns a lesson, and before you know it, your behavior has been changed in subtle ways.

Life is all about facing adversity and overcoming it. But when you shut out your inner voice—that inner part of yourself that must be heard—damage is done. Finding and listening to your inner voice[10] is easy once you recognize the real power that it has over you.

I like to call this your "hidden self" or your "true self," the part that is kept from the world and that is defended by your attitudes, beliefs, and behaviors. People often suppress who they really are out of fear, and it is this programmed fear response that ultimately makes us unhappy.

When you awaken from sleepwalking, you will be more dialed into your inner voice than ever before. This voice will guide you, inspire you, and give you the power to tell exactly what you really want from a situation at any given time. Life is about following the inspirations and intuitive messages that this inner voice gives you to unravel your own personal mystery.

This eventually answers the question "Who am I?" and leads to a fulfilled life. You are not your circumstances, and you are not your money, or your clothing, or your skinny waist, or your incredible skill with a tennis racket. Those are simply parts of your physical self. The hidden self, when fully exposed, influences your physical self.

The Process of Learning to Wake Up

Adversity is always preceded by choice, and this is when you need your hidden self to help you make those tough decisions. To expose

---

10   Dr. John F. Demartini, Listening to Your Guiding Whispers, http://healing.about.com/od/selfpower/a/wisdom_voice.htm

your hidden self,[11] the first step that you have to take is to learn about the process of waking up.

Knowing where you are in the grand scheme of your conscious and subconscious minds will help you determine what kind of work needs to be done to allow you to emerge from the sleepwalking state. It is easy to recede back into it if you allow yourself to do so!

I have identified four levels of connection that accurately define how aware an individual is of their hidden self. The more aware you are, the more awake you are—and being awake comes with greater control. When you are fully awake, you can consciously experience and influence exactly what your hidden self thinks, feels, and wants from the world.

The process of learning to awaken comes in these four stages:

Stage 1: Unconsciously Unaware

An unconsciously unaware person has no idea there is even a hidden self that is trying to communicate with them. They have no idea that they have subconscious blind spots that may be causing them harm. Self-destructive behavior may be rife, and extreme unhappiness, depression, or dissatisfaction can also be present.

The inner voice is completely ignored.

Stage 2: Consciously Unaware

A consciously unaware person understands that they have blind spots and weaknesses that they cannot seem to get over or repair. But they do not know why they feel so bad about them. Understanding about their own behavior is greatly limited, and they do not seek methods of fixing this obvious problem that they have in their lives.

The inner voice is heard but dismissed.

---

11   Henri Junttila, How to Hear Your Inner Wisdom When Making Tough Choices, http://tinybuddha.com/blog/hear-inner-wisdom-making-tough-choices/

Stage 3: Consciously Aware

A consciously aware[12] person recognizes that they have blind spots and weaknesses and has taken active steps to improve them. These individuals may be like you—they have picked up a book looking for some answers. In this stage, there is a lot of work to be done that involves balancing the key elements of your life.

The inner voice is heard and acted upon to a certain degree.

Stage 4: Unconsciously Aware

The unconsciously aware person is perfectly balanced and automatically recognizes their former blind spots and avoids them. They are fully invested in life balance and automatically consult their hidden selves to uncover the true meaning of things.

The inner voice is heard and is part of conscious decision-making.

The Unconsciously Unaware

The unconscious, or more accurately the subconscious, mind is like a storage room where all the information of your life has been stored. Previous life experiences, beliefs, memories, skills—everything you have ever done or seen is held here in this mystic vault.

When you move through life, it tends to flow in patterns. What you have learned before you perpetuate, and this is what causes cycles of similar behavior. Someone who was heartbroken as a young man may, for example, not be able to hold a relationship together because of mistrust—not because all of his partners were liars but because one was.

These stored feelings and memories shape how we behave, but they are not who we are. The subconscious mind can be reprogrammed. But first there has to be a realization somewhere along the line. As aforementioned, that inner voice is constantly trying to draw your attention to the fact that things are not okay and that you are on the wrong path.

---

12   Scott Leuthold, Understanding the Awakening Process, http://www.tokenrock.com/articles/understanding-the-awakening-process-68.html

The people that feel this most intrinsically are the unconsciously unaware.[13] These people do not know what they do not know or why. They are completely ignorant to their faults and are entirely unwilling to change any of their behaviors. They do not learn and are narrow minded. They believe that their way is the best way.

People may tell them that they are wrong all the time or that they are unpleasant, unhappy, and unhelpful—but these individuals simply ignore that. They are absorbed in the ego and chase material distractions of the physical self.

As this person moves through cycles of repetitive behavior, they may shift into the consciously unaware phase. But when they are still working through the unconsciously unaware phase, no one and nothing can tell them that they are wrong. The hidden self is so private that it is squashed down deep inside them.

This stage is most common when people are young and in their teen years. Many grow out of it and shift into other stages. Unfortunately, some people never do. Being unconsciously unaware can be dangerous. It can lead to a lot of self-destructive thinking, negative emotions, unhealthy relationships, and behaviors without any thought of the future or genuine internal needs and desires.

The outside world is everything, and the internal landscape is barren.

The Consciously Unaware

The next stage of awareness is when a person is consciously unaware. As life continues and similar circumstances recur, you may notice that similarly bad things keep happening to you. It is usually around this time that people begin to seek out new information, opportunities, and processes, which opens them up to change.

Suddenly, they begin to notice the faults inside themselves, and that inner voice gets a little louder. They start hearing it more often,

---

13 Unconsciously Unaware to Subconsciously Aware, http://www.alephsynergy.com/processes-awareness/Unconsciously-to-Subconsciously-aware.html

but they are afraid to act on it because it has been saying so many negative things. Remember, the inner chatter can be dangerous if left to its own learning patterns and devices.

Being conscious of the fact that something is wrong but unable to reach the point where you can do anything about it inspires guilt and, to a certain degree, increased levels of self-destructive behavior. There may be deep-seated feelings of unease or discomfort, a longing for change, but an unwillingness to take any necessary steps towards those goals.

In other words, the consciously unaware,[14] are conscious of their faults, but unaware of what it is that is causing them to act or feel as they do. They chalk it up to bad luck, poor circumstances, and bad relationships and blame other people for their unhealthy addictions and behaviors instead of looking inward. That inner voice becomes hostile because life becomes so challenging.

At this awareness level, you will start to notice that the things you have been doing have not been working in your favor. You may begin to realize that you need to go on a diet, for example, or that you should have a different friendship group.

This is the transition stage, and it can be the most turbulent. Living with an awareness that something is wrong with you is not easy, but it is a necessary cry for help that these individuals have to hear from within. One day you will simply begin to believe that there are better ways to do things.

These will circulate in your mind until you move on to the next stage of your awareness process. Acknowledging that there must be a better way to live or exist is a little step on a very long road to full awareness. The real work comes in when you reach the consciously aware stage.

---

14 Conscious and Competence, http://changingminds.org/explanations/learning/ consciousness_competence.htm

The Consciously Aware

Once you have reached the consciously aware stage, things start to change for you. Sometimes this change comes in thick waves and reshapes everything in your life. It all depends on what you were doing before this stage hit you.

By the time you become consciously aware of your faults and issues, you realize it is also solely up to you to change them. You suddenly realize that everything in your life has happened because of choices that you have made, and you are determined to get yourself back on track and to sort out some very real problems.

Consciously aware individuals are working towards balance in their lives. They have realized that it needs to happen in order for any sort of real authenticity and happiness to occur. Life balance means that they must adhere to their physical, mental, emotional, relational, and spiritual needs and take all five into account during any decision-making process.

Becoming consciously aware can take a while to get right as you transition from resisting balance to needing it more and more. Knowledge and guidance are two elements that can help you on your path, which is why this book will be so handy. You will be able to take leaps in conscious awareness and shift into unconscious awareness with these practices.

You will begin to notice other people who are listening to their inner selves and have become an example to you. You will learn from them and gravitate towards groups of people who have also realized that balance and spiritual acknowledgement is the only way to move forward and repair the damage that has been done from the division between your inner self and your outer self.

During this stage, you will be eager to drop bad habits and acquire new ones that are good for you. You will seek meaning in everything that you do and will observe and discover new perceptions—feeling inspired and exhilarated as you do. Life balance helps you feel in charge of life, like anything can happen—and this is the fundamental difference.

Unconscious unawareness feels like you are out of control on a runaway rollercoaster. Shifting into conscious awareness feels like you have become a superhero. The two sensations are entirely different, and you will quickly see why, in the end, the latter brings you fulfillment and happiness.

The Unconsciously Aware

When you reach the final stage of awareness, you will become unconsciously aware. This happens when you have practiced leading a balanced life so often that your inner voice and outer persona have become the same thing.

Then you will subconsciously act in your own best interest instead of subconsciously acting against your best interest. You will no longer allow your inner self to remain on autopilot. This is an incredibly powerful state, and it makes for happier, healthier people that lead full and productive lives.

Mastering continuous discovery in the pursuit of your purpose, of fulfillment, and of things that make you happy is something that can and must be programmed into your subconscious mind. This kind of auto pilot will make sure that whatever decision you make, it will be one that suits your best interest.

The unconsciously aware[15] are fiercely positive, well-rounded people that work hard on emotional stability, mental clarity, physical energy, manifesting supportive relationships, and spiritual wellness in everything they do. This means that they grow as whole human beings instead of people who concentrate on material pursuits and never find any real happiness in life.

---

15   The Conscious Competence Ladder, http://www.mindtools.com/pages/article/newISS_96.htm

The final stage of fulfillment is all about helping others achieve a similar sense of peace. It is the reason why I am writing this book and the reason why one day you will feel compelled to share this knowledge with someone else in your life.

With enough practice leading a healthy balanced life, you can reprogram the way your subconscious mind behaves and turn yourself into someone who can access their full potential. This divine potential is dormant in each of us and yearns to be expressed.

It is only when you have expressed this need and helped as many other people as possible with their own lives that you will strike the perfect life balance. When it is second nature to be your authentic self all the time, nothing could be better.

You will no longer have to think about yourself as two separate parts; you will be one whole being with a singular goal—your purpose. I have found throughout the years that this is the most desirable (and most difficult) state to reach, but it is possible.

Sleepwalking on a Tightrope

Now that you understand the levels that are ahead of you, perhaps you can come to terms with what you have been through. Life is not easy; you have discovered that. There are always obstacles to overcome and "tests" to get past.

There are good relationships and bad ones, money and poverty, and, of course, the endless cycle of doubt that exists within us all. Life is like a tightrope. When you are unconsciously unaware—or a sleepwalker—unfortunately, walking on that tightrope becomes close to impossible. Along the way, you are bound to fall many, many times.

It is the same reason why you have never been able to rise above your circumstances and blast out of your current environment or situation. You are only able to achieve what you currently know and understand.

When you are not even willing to admit that you are one of your biggest problems, then you will continue to walk along that tightrope fully asleep. But there is hope! With every drop to the ground, there is an opportunity and a challenge is posed.

It is the same reason why good things come from bad experiences or situations. During these dark times, we are forced to reassess our decisions. The universe tries to tell us this with every foot that we fall. The trick is to understand what life is and that you are giving up a huge part of it if you continue walking blindly along the tightrope.

The potential that lies within you will always want to be released. It will eat you up inside if you do not figure out a way to make it work. Once you have woken up, the tightrope walk will be easier. At least now you will be able to decide where your foot falls, when you step, and even where to grab if you suddenly drop off the edge.

This tightrope will extend before you for as long as you are alive. Life never stops being a challenge! But you can decide how you will meet that challenge. Will you meet it sleepwalking? Or will you meet it wide awake?

Personally, my money is on the wide awake folks. These are the people that will reach the end of this life fulfilled, happy, and grateful that they have been able to grace others with the key to the Life Balance existence.

Your Level of Waking Awareness

The first question for you then becomes—what is your level of awareness?

Are you like so many others, looking for quick fix solutions? Sorry, there are not any of those in this life. Tightropes begin, and they end. You cannot cheat your way across a tightrope. People that do often end up hanging themselves.

Self-awareness is a skill, as much as it is a condition. It needs to be identified, practiced, and eventually programmed into your mind. When you unify the subconscious and conscious minds and set them both on your life goals, nothing will stop you from achieving them.

You have exiled the inner part of yourself that was always meant to guide you towards your destined life path. You can plan and want a life that is different from the one that you have now, but this is still different from the life that you were meant to lead.

It is only when you are true to your authentic self that you can begin to experience the happiness and fulfillment involved in a balanced existence. Balance, as it is briefly translated, means getting many of the fundamentals right:

- Physical: Take care of all of your physical needs - **Be energized!**
- Mental: Notice your mental processes, change them if necessary, and practice constant self-awareness - **Be clear!**
- Emotional: Understand your internal feelings, and control your emotional state - **Be centered!**
- Interpersonal: Take note of your relationships, and make the necessary shifts to attract loving, supportive people - **Be connected!**
- Spiritual: Listen to your inner voice, and allow it to guide you beyond your own self-interests and accepting the present moment - **Be aligned!**

I want you to look in the mirror and address your inner self:

"I have been ignoring you for too long. It is time that we reunited and work together on leading a happier, healthier, more balanced life."

I am going to walk you through my many strategies for how to regain this unconscious awareness with the tightrope balance concept. You will learn how to embrace who you are and what you really want while you tend to your very basic needs.

Then you will discover why tending to these needs is critical as you search for people in your life to help. After all, balance has a social component, and what are we here for if not to help lift each other up to achieve our deepest purposes in life? Each of us has purpose; there are no coincidences, and we must all be observant to notice all the messages that come into our daily lives.

CHAPTER 3
THE OBSTACLES TO SELF-AWARENESS

"If your emotional abilities aren't in hand, if you don't have self-awareness, if you are not able to manage your distressing emotions, if you can't have empathy and have effective relationships, then no matter how smart you are, you are not going to get very far."
Daniel Goleman

There are many obstacles to self-awareness that you need to be aware of when forging ahead with your journey to finding an ideal life balance. They say that the first step to solving any lingering problem is to admit that there is one. Now that you have smashed through that starting point, the only things holding you back will be hidden parts of yourself.

No one ever said that self-awareness would be easy! There are many reasons why these obstacles hold us back and pull us back down to bad habits—and they are not always simple reasons. By understanding the obstacles, you can look out for them and avoid them along the long and winding path to better things.

The Trick with Self-Awareness

Getting to know yourself may sound confusing at first, but the truth is that too few people really take the time to understand who they are and what they want out of the world. You cannot have self-improvement without self-awareness. This means listening to that inner voice that lives inside even if you do not like what its saying.

The trick with self-awareness[16] is to focus on how you feel and what you need out of life. To get caught up too much in the smaller things can drive you crazy. Lines often get blurred, and this is not an exercise in vanity or ego. Self-awareness leads to selflessness. First you need to know what makes you happy and how to use that to help other people.

On this journey, there are many obstacles that will stand in your way. The hardest part is that you can bank on things becoming more difficult for you before they get better. You have been out of sync with yourself for so long that falling back in sync is going to be a battle.

During our lives, we all encounter psychological and emotional damage from childhood. Life, as I have mentioned, is a tightrope. When you are a child, you tend to fall more often and get hurt as you learn how things work in the world.

The trick here is to take note of these obstacles and remove them from the equation. Be mindful about their intrusion into your progress, and work to keep them at bay.

How to Deal With Universal Resistance

You have made a decision to change, and now the consequences of that decision will manifest in your life. I call this universal resistance because it relates directly to the onslaught of replacing old habits with new ones and reshaping your reality. Things are going to shift, and adversity is going to arise.

---

16   Thorin Klosowski, The Importance of Self-Awareness, and How to Become More Self Aware, http://lifehacker.com/the-importance-of-self-awareness-and-how-to-become-mor-1624744518

Resistance happens in small ways—like when you want to get outside and exercise but your favorite program just popped on TV. Things will constantly test your resolve in this life, and you have to be ready for it. There is even a neuroscience behind resistance in life. This is because you train your neural pathways to do something they enjoy doing, so they repeat it.

Your brain wants to travel on those pathways more often because it is comfortable. That is why if you are a depressive, it is so easy to become depressed. Your brain knows how and can easily access those areas without resistance. But with new behaviors and habits, the brain has to work doubly hard to build new pathways. There is discomfort, and it will look for ways to not have to do this!

That is why the moment you make a decision to change, it seems like the world rises up and prevents you from doing it. Ask anyone that has ever set a New Year's resolution! Universal resistance is real because it happens the moment you decide you want change in your life. This is a big obstacle and one you have to learn how to overcome.

- Understand that resistance[17] is normal. Accept those feelings and acknowledge the distractions and temptations. Always choose to continue practicing and repeating the new, desired habit or action to improve things anyway.

- To untangle from the mess of resistance, set rules for yourself. Limit your distractions, and take a hard line approach to change. For example, today I will run three miles, and nothing will stop me from doing it. Plan this time carefully so that the least resistance happens and you can actively get the action in.

- Understand how resistance feels, and begin to recognize it when it happens. This is a powerful one and already taps into your inner voice for intuitive recognition. When resistance is

17   Elisha Goldstein, Ph.D., The Neuroscience of Resistance and How to Overcome It!, http://blogs.psychcentral.com/mindfulness/2014/09/the-neuroscience-of-resistance-and-how-to-overcome-it/

happening, you will feel pressure and temptation, excuses will start circulating in your mind, and you will feel tired or long for something else. These are all brain tricks to keep you distracted from hard work.

Impulsive Thinking vs. Committed Thinking

Your thoughts are what govern your behaviors, so before you can master how you act, you need to be aware of how you think. That is why the next biggest obstacle to achieving life balance is understanding the difference between impulsive and committed thinking.

If you think about it, failure usually results because you do things without thinking about them first or you think about things without doing them. Whatever your approach, there is no denying that your thoughts are essential to the process. Here is the difference between these two methods of thought:

- **Impulsive thinking:** When your thoughts jump[18] around and do whatever they wish, leaping from one negative thing to another or to a positive thing—without any conscious control on your part—these are impulsive thoughts. They usually lead to impulsive actions and definitely need to be self-regulated.

  For example: You have had a bad week. You have been mindlessly dwelling on all the bad things that have happened, and you feel trapped. Because of your impulsive thoughts, you feel bad about yourself—has it all been your fault? To feel better, you decide to go out and drink with a group of friends and end up driving home drunk.

- **Committed thinking:** When your thoughts are carefully selected and controlled because you know how powerful they can be, these are committed thoughts. You are consciously

---

18   Dr. George Simon, Impulsive Thinking, Impulsive Actions, Dire Consequences, http://counsellingresource.com/features/2008/12/29/impulsive-thinking/

aware that you must not dwell on negatives and instead focus your thoughts around positive goals and stop negative thought cycles in their tracks.

For example: You have had a challenging week. But you have not allowed your mind to dwell on negative thoughts, so you still feel good about yourself. Because you have been focused on a positive goal, you feel inspired to make next week better. You go out with friends and have a great time without drinking alcohol while planning your upcoming vacation.

Impulsive thinking drives negative emotions and bad decision-making, while committed thinking drives positive emotions and good decision-making. The distinction between the two is simple. But practicing committed thought is a challenge. Remember resistance? You will encounter it as you attempt to change how you think about your life and the world.

The Human Ego: Always Right

The human ego can be a dangerous thing. If you cannot see past it, it can cause you a lot of grief and adversity. This is because ego is the thing that makes you feel separate and apart from the rest of the universe. It singles you out and wants special attention all the time.

Ego[19] is intensely related to how we feel when we interact with other people. It is the thing that allows us to feel important or feel neglected at any given time. Ego can often be the root of all conflict and can spark many challenges that you will have to face.

The human ego, however, is a fragile thing. I am not asking you to give it up or suppress it but rather to be conscious of how yours functions in your life. An ideal state is to coexist with your ego but be able to put it aside when it is preventing you from moving forward. Your ego will tell you that you are always right, but logically, that is not true all the time.

---

19   Dr. Sircus, The Ego as the Root of All Conflict, http://drsircus.com/personal/the-ego-as-the-root-of-conflict

Narcissists are created when ego becomes dysfunctional. They believe everything and everyone in the world exists to serve them, and they seek absolute control. This means that with anyone else, they will constantly be at loggerheads. It is far better to train your ego[20] so that it can be used for your benefit instead of hindrance.

- Get used to switching places with people in a mental and emotional sense. Adopt their point of view, and try to recognize the truth in a situation, whatever that may be. By putting your ego aside, you will arrive at the right perspective, which is helpful.

- Avoid the negative feelings associated with regret and pride. Try not to feel bad about anything that you discover about yourself. Instead, seek to change the parts of yourself that you dislike so that you do not have to feel that way. Be proud of your achievements but not overly so. Pride can be a downfall, especially when it gets in the way of humility and service.

- Focus on your outer and inner experience. Your spirit can tell what is happening if you only take the time to practice silence and to listen. Reflect on what is happening, and find out how you can progress or learn from it as a human being. Accept the behavior of others, but never judge them—these traits also lie in you.

The Critic Within: It Lies

People lie all the time. It would astound you just how much you lie to yourself. When the inner self does not know something, it often pretends to know so that it can have something to say or think about that subject. But the truth is that a lot of internal dialogue is just a pack of lies. We talk about things that we do not know about as though we do know them.

---

20 Strategies to Overcome Ego, http://humanscience.wikia.com/wiki/Strategies_to_
overcome_ego

Of course this is only the tip of the iceberg. That inner voice has a nasty side, and I am sure that you have heard and felt it. When you say negative, critical, and nasty things to yourself, over and over again, sometimes your conscious mind begins to believe them.

Because you have trained your brain to be negative and to cycle through negative thoughts about yourself, you are feeding yourself a never ending pack of lies[21] about who you are, what you are, and what you could be. These are all self-limiting behaviors, and they need to stop. These obstacles will keep you from doing the most basic things in life.

Depression is a great example. A person that is depressed constantly feels hatred or sadness about themselves. They feel worthless, that life is meaningless, and that things will never get any better. They have told themselves this so many times that they now feel it all of the time and cannot shake it.

Due to this, they struggle to get up in the morning. They do not bathe, or eat, or work, or even speak to other people. This is what can happen when the critic within is left to run wild through your life. The thing is, that critic is lying. Nothing that it is saying is true.

Things can, and will, get better, and by all accounts, if that person still has skills, they can make a success of themselves whenever they choose to. They have just forgotten that they have a choice. They have been trapped in the negative self-talk for so long that it has become a part of their reality.

So negative self-talk needs to be ignored and actively changed. When it says something inside that hurts or feels bad, reject it. Choose to believe the opposite or to at least say the opposite out loud. Your inner critic is a liar and wants to strip you of your divine power. It has been exposed to the world too long and isolated from your conscious mind.

---

21   Seven Primary Obstacles to Self-Awareness, http://gaiancorps.com/study/psychology-mind/fourth-way/the-basics/item/29-seven-primary-obstacles-to-self-awareness

Without any guidance the critic/liar has become a mechanism for despair, sadness, and anger. You need to work on that and change it back into a mechanism for joy, happiness, and peace. Be conscious of the lies that you tell yourself all the time. Put a stop to that sad feeling you feel when you lie to yourself. They are all unnecessary!

Self-Responsibility Mountain: Climbing High

Self-awareness cannot exist without personal responsibility. At some point in your life, perhaps right now, you have recognized that you are responsible for your actions, your thoughts, and the reality that has resulted from them. I want to impress upon you just how important this is for your personal development.

Self-responsibility is a steep mountain, and you are going to have to climb very high to reach the peak. This means that you are directly responsible, answerable, and accountable[22] for your progress with self-awareness and achieving life balance. No one is going to hold your hand as you think that negative thought again.

No one is going to stop you from making that awful decision born out of self-destructive behavior. Only you have the will and discipline required to change direction and pursue this new state of being. Switching from a negative life to a positive one is probably the most difficult thing that you will ever do.

The rewards, however, are far beyond anything you could possibly imagine. Not only will you be healthier and happier but you will also be a more authentic version of yourself. You will understand your purpose and will be able to live each day meaningfully while applying yourself in the right areas—where you are most useful and happy.

Self-responsibility[23] is one of the biggest obstacles in awakening

---

22 Accepting Personal / Self Responsibility, http://www.theawarenessparty.com/links-and-resources/articles/scientific/spontaneous-evolution/accepting-personal-self-responsibility/

23 Self-Awareness and Personal Responsibility, http://www.sosoft.com/blog/2011/06/06/self-awareness-and-personal-responsibility/

from your sleepwalk. This is because you will stumble and fall a few times before you get it right. Most people just do not have the discipline to pick themselves up and keep moving along the right path.

- You are responsible for the things that you think. If you mess up, you are responsible for trying again—as many times as is needed to succeed. It is inevitable that with more practice, you will train yourself to be positive and empowered; the rest is a matter of working through the obstacles and sticking to your plan.

- You are responsible for the things that you do. If you make a mistake, cast away the negative feelings of doubt and failure. They will not help you achieve anything. Instead, start over, and give yourself a pep talk. Everyone stumbles, but even when you stumble, you can successfully reach the end of the path.

There is a mountain ahead of you. Expect rock fall, cold nights, rainy days, and difficult climbing. Trust yourself to reach the top by never giving up. You will succeed.

Building Internal Barriers

There are many internal barriers to self-awareness that you may come across as you walk along this journey. These barriers have built up over time and have imprisoned your potential so that it is locked away deep inside.

Fear and doubt are the two biggest barriers, and they lead to all sorts of negative feelings that will keep you from achieving a true life balance. Watch out for these feelings and thoughts, and actively cast them from your mind. You can also replace them with more positive thoughts and actions that you can create yourself.

- If you do not feel "good enough" or you feel like an imposter, this is simply worry and anxiety manifesting from internalized doubt and fear. This barrier can keep you from experiencing the satisfaction and success you deserve.

- Achievement is not the result of "getting lucky." It is a direct response to hard work, planning, and time investment. Convincing yourself that you have had success because you were "just lucky" is a lie. This is an internal barrier that denies you the right to feel proud of your achievements.

- Reach out to other people for support. When you begin to feel like an internal barrier of fear is keeping you from doing something, tell someone close to you. Trust them with your feelings, and ask for advice. Friends can affirm your successes and alchemize your failures. They reflect your true reality back to you.

- Build visions of your future. The inner voice inside you loves to dream, especially of the future that you could have. Invest time in visualizing your ideal future or visualizing overcoming a specific barrier—and then work towards achieving it. Goal fulfillment pleases the inner voice more than anything else.

Internal barriers[24] need to be pulled down, which means stepping outside your comfort zone. You will know when you reach those points because you will not feel "good enough," or a number of other negative feelings will stir inside you. Remember, only your inner self truly knows what you are capable of. You can do the most extraordinary things!

As you repeat positive things back to yourself and hear about your true successes from your friends, it will help you bring down those internal barriers. Gain confidence in your ability, cast away doubt and fear, and embrace the bravery you once had as a young child. We all need this courage to make great things happen in our lives.

---

24 Tips for Overcoming Internal Barriers to Success, http://lifepluswork.com/tips-for-overcoming-internal-barriers-to-success/

This Is What You Are: A Point of Perspective

The timeless question that has been asked since the dawn of time by every human that has ever lived has been, who am I? This is not a question that can be answered but rather a question that poses a challenge. Who do you want to be?

The whos and whats of life are simple when you break them down and look at what they really mean in the life of an individual. While your tastes and perspectives may change, that inner being, that spirit inside you, already knows what you are.

- What do you believe in? Beliefs are a powerful thing. Your perspective on what you believe helps shape who and what you are.

- What do you love to do, think, and experience? List the things in life that you love to do, think, and experience the most out of anything else. This can tell you a lot about what your spirit is attracted to and what you need from this world.

- What do you dislike the most? Which things in this world do you not like to do, think, or experience? These are the things that would make you the unhappiest, so be sure to steer clear of them at all costs.

- Your ethics and values matter. How you feel about morality and the values that you have makes up a significant portion of who you are.

You are more than the sum total of your physical appearance, your skills, your manners, and your outlook on life. Deep inside, there is a hunger - to help others in a specific way. This is what you are, and you should spend a good amount of time in your life finding that out.

I found out at a very young age that I was meant to counsel other people through hard times. My own difficult experiences taught me how to help people through some of the most challenging times of their lives, which gave me enormous happiness.

The what that I became over many years of practice was a counselor and a teacher. The who...well, that is still a work in progress. Perspective is a powerful thing. When you realize that there is no single answer, things change. To your mother, you are a son. To a shopkeeper, you are a customer. Who you are is who you are driven to be inside.

In psychology, it is called the "self-concept,"[25] and it is constantly in progress.

25 Saul McLeod, Self Concept, http://www.simplypsychology.org/self-concept.html

PART II

WALKING DOWN ENLIGHTENED PATHS

CHAPTER 4
THE SIDEWALK CONCEPT

"Follow your bliss, and the universe will open doors where there were only walls."

Joseph Campbell

The second part of this book takes a look at walking down enlightened paths. Now that you have realized there is an awakening process that needs to jar you out of your sleepwalk, I want to help you understand why. An enlightened path is very different from one shrouded in darkness. Only one of them ever shows you a clear path to happiness.

I want to put the tightrope analogy aside for now and move to another. Perhaps by using this analogy you will finally see why sleepwalking down your life path is unwise. I call it the "sidewalk concept," and it is a great way of explaining how the human mind works when it does not know where it is going or where your next footstep will fall.

There is a poem that I love to use in my practice when counseling people and teaching them about the merits of moving from being asleep to being awake in this world. It is called "There's a Hole in My Sidewalk" by Portia Nelson.[26]

The poem speaks about the various levels of awareness that a human being can possess. Sleepwalking, you are bound to fall into the same holes again and again, but once you begin to open your eyes, change can happen. Eventually, you not only spot the problem but you find a way around it. You change your own destiny and prevent cycles of misfortune and bad habits from impacting your future.

The Core Problem: What Hole?

Life, you may have noticed, is ever-changing yet strangely consistent. It raises a lot of questions and is a mystery to most people. When you factor in levels of self-awareness, this becomes much clearer. The core problem, you see, is that most people do not even see the holes. Let me give you an example.

A father of two kids who has been married for 12 years has serious anger problems that stem from childhood trauma. His marriage is failing, and he comes to me for help. Instantly, I notice that anger is impacting every behavior and action that this man takes. He does not even realize he is an angry person. He cannot see the "hole" because it is his normal.

What if I told you that stress is killing you in ways you do not even realize right now. Limited awareness is far more costly to your physical, emotional, interpersonal, mental, and spiritual states than you may think. Try having a healthy relationship when you cannot see your faults! Modern-day stress causes darkness; it keeps us looking outside instead of inward.

---

26   Poem: There's a Hole in My Sidewalk, http://mymeditativemoments.com/realization-for-change/

Some forms of stress[27] are good for you and can improve brain function and creativity as well as make you fit—under the right circumstances. But on the whole, chronic stress causes overloading on a daily basis, and it sabotages your health and wellbeing. Stress-related diseases are everywhere, and that is not a coincidence.

The physical aspect of stress can be measured with modern-day science. Until stress is adequately released, it remains lodged in your body, causing your cells to run rampant. Do not believe me? Think about a recently stressful situation. Work stress, money issues, relationship trouble, or family unrest—what has changed?

Your body has begun to respond to anxiety and worry. Your energy is being depleted, you begin to procrastinate about things, and health issues crop up. This is because your amygdala in your midbrain senses danger and your "fight or flight" response lights up. Your body kicks into gear, releasing adrenaline and the stress hormone cortisol.

Blood is diverted away from your digestive tract so that you cannot absorb food effectively. Nutrient uptake slows, and weight gain increases. In this heightened state, all non-essential systems shut down. You struggle to solve problems, your creative skills wane, and your intuition suffers. You begin to feel irritable, isolated, and impatient.

Not only do your relationships suffer but you cannot sleep, your health takes a knock (immune system reduction and rise in blood pressure), and you slip into adrenal fatigue. Depression and exhaustion begin to feel normal. With no energy, you stop exercising, eating properly, and looking after yourself. Pain, insomnia, and other concerns crop up.

Stress makes you blind to the holes in your life by crippling your internal systems.

---

27   The Effects of Stress on the Body, http://www.healthline.com/health/stress/effects-on-body

The Five Bad Habits That Keep Us in the Dark

If you cannot see the holes that prevent you from walking along your true life path, guess what? You are going to keep falling into them. Instead of walking around them or finding a new road to walk down, you end up in cycles of bad behavior that negatively impact the core areas that make you a healthy human being.

Imagine that you have a destiny but that it is at the end of a long, winding road. This road is called "life." But because you are sleepwalking, you are completely in the dark. Every time you set out to find your way along the road, you stumble into a hole. Then you have to figure out how to climb out of it. Some people do but very, very few of them.

The more likely outcome is that each time you fall into the hole, you climb out, only to fall back in again at another point down the road. When you are sleepwalking through life, you just cannot see the dangers ahead. This exposes your physical, mental, emotional, relational, and spiritual side to attack all the time.

When stress attacks and things go wrong in life, we often wonder what has happened. We blame circumstances, friends, and family. We search for something other than ourselves to hold accountable. But accountability can only come from awareness,[28] and that begins inside you. A sleepwalking man can blame a hole for being there, but the hole is not going to move.

The only movable part of the equation is the person. He has to figure out that the path is more serious than he previously believed to be true—that there are real dangers and he must prepare for them. Lots of things in life keep people in the dark aside from stress. When you sleepwalk through life, a lot escapes your understanding and narrows your field of view.

---

28 Self-Awareness – The Key to Breaking Bad Habits, http://www.mind-awakening-techniques.com/self-awareness-bad-habits.php

There are five bad habits that are especially damaging, and I want you to shake these off as quickly as you can. The first step is understanding them then practicing them for yourself. If you can change your outlook, you can begin to blink your eyes open to see what lies ahead.

- Habit #1: Investing in the belief that reality is objective
- Habit #2: Failure to disconnect emotionally and separate from your un-resourceful current experience
- Habit #3: Focusing on the negative aspects of life while investing in a victimhood mentality
- Habit #4: Failure to recognize the need for real-life balance
- Habit #5: Being completely resistant to change

In the next few pages, we will take a closer look at what each of these five habits mean in your life and how you can rid yourself of them to finally wake up!

Your Objective Reality: Stuck in the Hole

The first bad habit that keeps you locked into the pattern of falling into holes along your path is to invest in the belief that reality is objective. I have never understood why people insist on attempting to reach some kind of bizarre consensus so that we can all agree that the world is the same for all of us and that we can see it objectively.

Consider the raw absurdity of this thought. You never really see the events of your life directly as they are. You always see them through a filter that distorts them, deletes them, or generalizes them. Human beings are like computers—we input, output, and process information about the territory around us.

All the information around us is soaked up, and we code it in terms of the five senses—sight, hearing, smell, touch, and taste. And experts cannot even agree on that. Some claim that people have as many as 21 senses[29]; we simply do not understand them well enough yet. This language of the human body is the most advanced system of experience in the world. Specialists have theorized that our eyes see less than one billionth of all the stimuli in any given moment in time. None of these stimuli get processed consciously. A psychological example of just how subjective our lives are can be found in the existence of scotoma. A mental scotoma is the failure to see something directly in front of your eyes.

It happens because you simply do not expect to see it. People delete out what they do not want to see. A very common example of this centers around the "missing keys" experience we have all enjoyed. You may search in earnest for 20 minutes and find your keys in a highly visible spot on the table.

The idea that any two people could view or experience the same situation from two distinctly different perspectives is ludicrous. Personal life experience is all that matters, and this is a subjective reality, not an objective one! We subjectively[30] interpret and add meaning to our own worlds. To make it even more complex, consider that your experience is not a true representation either. "The map is not the world" as Alfred Korzybski once said.

You organize your world through your senses, perceptual filters, and past recollections. Reality is only a mirror of your expectations. So believing that life is objective and "set in stone" is a very limiting belief indeed.

Emotional Disconnection: Not a Bad Thing at All

Second on the list of unhelpful practices is the very human habit of connecting everything to our own emotional experiences. Often the emotional and physical attachments that we have in our lives govern

29   Daven Hiskey, Humans Have a Lot More Than Five Senses, http://www. todayifoundout.com/index.php/2010/07/humans-have-a-lot-more-than-five-senses/
30   Ed Diener, Richard Lucas, Subjective Well-Being, http://greatergood.berkeley.edu/images/application_uploads/Diener-Subjective_Well-Being.pdf

our lives. Take a moment to consider which things in your life you absolutely could not live without.

You may have instantly thought of a loved one, a significant other, or perhaps your regular use of alcohol or tobacco. Maybe you cannot live without your favorite television programs or your use of the Internet on the computer. If you could not live without any of these things, you are in fact over-attached.

While being over-attached is normal with human relationships, not being able to separate yourself and your emotions from other things can be damaging. Imagine if your favorite television show was abruptly cancelled. Would you be in a bad mood? Or worse yet, imagine if a new law was passed banning alcohol. How would you survive that?

Emotions are meant to help you and connect you to things, but they can also be a roadblock on your path to enlightenment and self-awareness. Intense emotions that cause a physical reaction for what should be small and insignificant is not healthy. This is even true in relationships. Fighting about whose turn it is to load the dishwasher is a bad thing.

Being overly emotional[31] all the time can cause significant dysfunction in life, especially if you feel so strongly about things, places, and experiences that are ultimately not important. People assign importance and meaning to things, but this can cause a lot of black holes.

I am not advocating for you to become an emotionally detached person. I am simply saying that being overly attached to things emotionally can cause harm and limitations. There is a real art to "letting go" and staying calm about things in life. Dropping a cup and breaking it should not be an emotionally turbulent experience. This causes stress, and I have already explained what that does to your body and mind.

---

31 Remez Sasson, Emotional Detachment for a Better Life, http://www. successconsciousness.com/books/emotional-detachment-for-better-life.html

Sparing yourself the physical, mental, and emotional energy of becoming upset, angry, or sad about things that do not matter is an important part of "waking up." You will never find inner peace if your external world impacts you so heavily. Learning to filter and control these connections is key to stabilizing your emotions.

Focus Pocus: Wishing Yourself a Victim

The third bad habit and one of my own personal favorites is what I like to call "focus pocus" because when you truly change it, it can seem like magic.[32] Where you happen to focus your attention, whether positive or negative, tends to be where your focus likes to go. This is why most people are trapped in a negative mindset!

Unfortunately for these people, despite the fact that countless research studies have proven that maintaining a negative world view is ultimately damaging to your physical, mental, and emotional health, people still love to see the glass half empty. And when I say "love," I mean it literally. The brain enjoys walking along pathways that on a chemical level it finds to be easy.

So the more negative you are, the more negative you become. A small amount of negative thinking opens the floodgates to larger amounts of negative thinking. Life constantly teaches us that whether we believe we can do something or we believe we cannot, we will make it come true. A simple but profound piece of wisdom that I share with my clients states: "We prove in life what we believe rather than believing what we prove."

Remember the last time you sank into a chair and thought "Why me?" Those good reasons that you thought were viable were only a product of your own negative mindset. When you wish yourself the victim, you become one. No one is to blame but you for life outcomes.

Too many people suffer from an un-resourceful belief system that takes this occasional belief a step further—your internal dialogue gets

---

32   Kate Corbin, The Magic of Focus, http://www.selfgrowth.com/articles/the-magic-of-focus

stuck on a loop. "Why me?" becomes "Bad things always happen to me!" and so they do. The statement alone presupposes that this type of experience will come true because you will continue to be victimized by the world.

Investing in this kind of limited reality only serves one purpose—it sends our minds on an unconscious search to find evidence that supports this dysfunctional, subjective way of seeing the world. In an ironic twist, the very experience that we want to transcend—the fear of being victimized—becomes a self-imposed reality.

You have to be careful what you spend energy avoiding in life because you may indirectly create it. St. Vincent De Paul knew this wisdom to be true when he said, "Make it a practice to judge persons and things in the most favorable light at all times, in all situations." You are who you practice being. You think what you practice thinking. It is focus pocus magic.

An Unbalanced Perspective: Your Failure

You are failing at something fundamental, big time. The good news is that a lot of this book is about setting that straight. The fourth habit that needs to be broken before you attain self-awareness concerns balance—life balance to be exact. Every human being on the planet functions at different levels.

Have you ever wondered what makes some people high functioning and others not? When your life is in balance, your body, mind, and spirit work in unison for your benefit. When life becomes out of balance, this is when dysfunction happens. Try aligning yourself to be balanced, and see how much difference it makes in your life.

The healing power of achieving a steady life balance is evident in your perspective. For example, when you look after your physical side, you feel energetic and are better able to handle the stressors of external daily living. When you are overweight, sickly, and eat junk food all day, you cannot expect to be making good decisions about yourself or for yourself.

The same can be said with the mental side of things because they bleed into each other. With an unhealthy body, your mind will not be able to cope with the reduction in function. Thoughts will be foggy and unclear, and you will struggle to make decisions that best benefit you. Mental health, however, is a must-have for anyone looking to step into self-awareness.

Once your body and mind are working well, you will need to take a look at your emotional side. As I mentioned earlier, a lot of dysfunction can arise in this area. With your mind playing tricks on you and your body producing chemicals that make you feel a certain way, the odds of you controlling your emotions when the other two are not aligned are slim.

Then there is your interpersonal side, or relational side, as I like to call it. People impact you on every level all the time. They are the main sources of the conflict and love that we deal with in daily life. You will not be able to handle social interaction correctly if your emotional, physical, and mental sides are out of line. Think about how being "hungry" changes your attitude!

Finally, there is your spiritual[33] side—an often repressed but vital portion of yourself that wants to be healed. This is where your consciousness and internal voice live. Take care of the other aspects of what it means to be a human being, and you will gain deeper access to your spirituality, which means happiness, fulfillment, and calm will be possible. Imagine that!

The Change Monster: It Is Behind You

The fifth and final bad habit that you need to shake is about being resistant to change. The idea that you could not like change is silly and comes from objective world perceptions. Nothing ever stays the same, and change in everyday life—however small—is inevitable. But people basically fear the unknown, so change becomes something to fight off.

---

33 Jasmin Tanjeloff, How to Create a Balanced Life: 9 Tips to Feel Calm and Grounded, http://tinybuddha.com/blog/9-tips-to-create-a-balanced-life/

This "change monster" seems to enter their lives and offer opportunities that they just do not want to handle. Even though a young man might be offered an exciting job with excellent compensation, it does not mean he will take it. The negative mind will find reasons why going would be a giant mistake. Change becomes an instant threat, an intolerable one.

Change always[34] lies ahead of us, just like it has been behind us all along. If your internal battles against life's changes become frequent, it can get very easy to feel out of control and stuck in an un-resourceful mindset. Mental "ruts" are the deepest holes of all!

They keep you clambering to get out of the hole for much, much longer than it should take to simply climb out of it. People become familiar with their bad attitudes and behaviors; it does not matter how unhappy or dissatisfied they might be. The tragedy of the human condition is that you can adapt to being miserable and embrace it without even knowing why.

When you personally believe that your own subjective truth is objective reality and emotionally become attached to that idea or feeling, it can cause intense unhappiness. This is that "trapped" feeling that many people get. They know their instincts are screaming for change, but the fear is so great they cannot consider it.

The irony, of course, is that they are already living in the misery that they fear will happen. People end up manifesting the thing that they fear the most—being a consummate victim. This breeds continual resentment, and gradually they withdraw from life, avoiding change wherever it may be—even though it offers them a ladder out of the hole.

Remember that change is not only possible but it is inevitable. Each of us really are the authors of our own destinies. You are not a victim of your life circumstances! Your thoughts, words, and deeds create a present experience that later becomes your future.

---

34   Rosabeth Moss Kanter, Ten Reasons People Resist Change, https://hbr.org/2012/09/ten-reasons-people-resist-chang.html

CHAPTER 5
ACRES OF DIAMONDS

"Life is one big road with lots of signs. So when you're riding through the ruts, don't complicate your mind. Flee from hate, mischief and jealousy. Don't bury your thoughts, put your vision to reality. Wake Up and Live!"
Bob Marley

Your life can be anything you want it to be. Have you heard this before? Hearing it and experiencing it are two completely different things. As a counselor who has worked with thousands of patients, I have seen this concept in action many times. Without fail, the people that recover from sleepwalking are the ones that take this information to heart.

Where you are now…is your fault. A better way of saying this is that you have created your own reality. Every hard decision that you have made has led you to where you are. It is a reflection of what your minimum standards really are because most people only act on what they cannot live without. This chapter will reveal some incredible things to you.

An African Tale

Have you ever heard the true story called "acres of diamonds"? I like to use this story to highlight a very specific problem that we all have in life. See if you can spot it.

This is an African tale set in the mid-1800s. Russell Conwell[35] was an educator and a minister, and he was approached by his church to assist some of its congregation with getting them into college. Conwell became very passionate about creating opportunities for poor folks to get formally educated. He spent a lot of years raising millions of dollars to establish Temple University. Eventually, he achieved his goals, giving 6,000 free lectures to people, telling them this African tale:

Once there was a farmer who was excited about prospecting for diamonds in Africa. He spent his entire life in a vain pursuit for wealth but never found it. Despondent, the man threw himself into the river and drowned.

A new owner stepped in and took over his property. No, not the property that could have diamonds on it but the one the original owner vacated in order to seek his diamond fortune. This man discovered a large crystal in the stream there and placed it prominently on the mantle of his fireplace. Later, a visitor recognized the crystal, and do you know what it was?

It was the largest diamond to have ever been found on the African continent. The diamond was simply in raw form. The new owner turned the farm into today's most productive diamond mine on the African continent. The moral here is clear: the first farmer spent his whole life looking elsewhere for what he already had at home—acres of diamonds!

We all stand amidst our own acres of diamonds. You just need to have the courage to look at your present moment, to notice them,

---

35   Russell H. Conwell, Acres of Diamonds, http://www.gutenberg.org/files/368/368-h/368-h.htm

and to take action. Most people never see them, and even fewer act on them.

The Sidewalk Process: Spotting Holes

One of the key issues with transitioning from a sleepwalking state to one of being "wide awake" and self-aware concerns your ability to spot holes. In other words, you need to understand how the sidewalk process works.

During the very first level of self-awareness, you are completely blind. Your conscious and subconscious minds are fast asleep, and you wander into any hole ahead of you. Those holes can be related to any of the five key areas (body, mind, emotions, interpersonal, and spirit), and they cause havoc in your life.

When you are sleepwalking into holes, it continues this way forever. Each time you fall in and blame others, it takes ages to climb out. Each time you stumble into the same holes. For example, a person at risk for contracting diabetes will eventually do so if they continue to eat badly and gain weight. As each year passes, worse things will happen because the core "hole" or problem was never fixed.

At the second most basic level, you have recognized your key hole areas. Continuing with the diabetes analogy, you know that you need to eat better, exercise more, work on your stress, and not drink so much alcohol. All of these areas are pressing, but you choose to ignore them. You fall into the holes again and again. Most people are here until they take the step to the next level.

Once you reach the next phase, you not only notice the holes[36] but you have seen how they transpire into the consequences you face. Your eyes are open. You know you are going to end up in the hospital if you continue to eat badly and not exercise. You recognize these

---

36   Dirk de Bruin, Simplify Your Life by Eliminating These 7 Problems, http://tinybuddha.com/blog/simplify-your-life-by-eliminating-these-7-problems/

basic truths and are able to recover from your mistakes a lot more quickly. Change happens.

As you change your behavior, you learn to walk around the holes. You only fall in occasionally—but you know that they are there, so for the most part, you can skirt around them. As time goes by, you learn to walk down another street altogether. There are no holes there, so you are in no danger anymore.

Everyone has to move through these levels to become self-aware and to gain the ability to process where their issues lie and how to fix them. That is what self-awareness is—the ability to perceive your problems and correct them with change.

The Three Fundamentals: Open Your Eyes

Opening your eyes can be a gradual process. The goal is to eventually achieve full balance in life. As you have seen, one area of your "being" impacts the other areas, and the only real way to compensate is to try to live a balanced, well-rounded life.

I have spent years developing systems that have helped my clients find their way to happiness through self-awareness, and I really consider it a super power to have. Once you have awakened from the sleepwalk, you will never be caught off guard by your own personal faults again. But you must continue working on repairing them.

This is self-improvement and self-healing[37] at its most powerful. Sometimes, depending on the patient, it can be one main problem that is feeding the rest and throwing them off balance. Sometimes it is a host of problems, from a past childhood trauma or a bad experience. Whatever the instigator, these internal mechanisms of dysfunction can be resolved.

All it takes is a commitment to the principle of self-awareness. Living with your eyes open means living the best life you can, with your own pitfalls, negative behaviors, and issues in mind. When you

---

37   Self Healing Process, http://www.spiritual-healing-for-you.com/self-healing-process.html

begin to work through them, you reduce the stress that they place on your life, and you start to heal. Powerful things will happen to you during this process.

That is why there are three fundamental elements involved in the process of attaining self-awareness. These help you to recognize or "see" all the "holes" and to break through the unawareness that has shaped you into the person that you are today.

These barriers need to be torn down if you are going to recover. For this reason, I have built a three-phase process for you to follow— the new solution framework, which includes learning how to wake up from your sleepwalk, advice on not falling down any rabbit holes, and, finally, how to use your personal energy to advance and succeed.

Once I have moved you through the three-step process, you will feel like a whole new person. Revitalized, positive, and ready for any challenge, you will be able to face life with renewed vigor. Challenging your habits, behaviors, and actions is never easy, but the rewards are worth it. Today is the day that you learn to open your eyes and self-heal!

Phase 1: The New Solution Framework

I have a new solution framework to offer you as your first step towards waking up. As I explained, the first tiny step that you take towards opening your eyes on that tightrope, or along that well-trodden path, is to be able to see your obstacles or challenges.

You will have obvious problems that other people have pointed out, but this book is not about other people; it is about you. And you know yourself best. That is why my new solution framework teaches you how to wake up to yourself via health and wellness.

Before mental clarity, emotional stability, relational improvement, or spiritual enrichment, physical health is of primary importance. It impacts and influences all the other areas of our being in dramatic ways. Do you not believe me?

Do you ever get home from work after a long drive and end up in a fight with your spouse? Many people have, and some people make a habit of it. This is not because you have been waiting all day to verbally attack them; it is because your physical body has been trapped in a car for over an hour. Slowly, your levels of irritability increase.

Then, because you are usually alone in your car, you will begin to reflect on all the negative things that have happened in your day. Moment by moment your body becomes more alarmed. It is the reason why road rage is a real problem and why when you step into your house after a long time sitting in traffic, you need to calm down and unwind.

The physical stress that you have placed on your body is not healthy. This stress then filters through to all other areas of your being until—like a grenade—you explode. All stress needs an exit or it is transferred from one location to the next. Most of the time it creeps up on you disguised as something else.

Knowing when this physical stress[38] is getting to you is as simple as listening to your body. Yes, you should be healthy. No, you should not be overweight or unfit. When your body is in good shape, it deals with physical stressors—like being stuck in traffic—that much better. My new solution framework will show you how to focus on your health and dial down the stress impact.

Phase 2(a): Down the Rabbit Hole

The second part of the three-step process is to avoid falling down any un-resourceful rabbit holes. You may not have realized it yet, but we all live with a certain amount of past emotional pain and trauma. Some people are oblivious to theirs and keep it well away from their current lives, while others choose to revisit this pain often.

---

38   Stress: How to Cope Better With Life's Challenges, http://familydoctor.org/familydoctor/en/prevention-wellness/emotional-wellbeing/mental-health/stress-how-to-cope-better-with-lifes-challenges.html

Every negative[39] or painful experience is a mental rabbit hole. You choose when to slide down those rabbit holes and indulge in the feelings that lie within. Because modern-day life has become so stressful, unfortunately, it has our natural trigger mechanisms confused.

You are mentally wired to notice negativity so that you can avoid danger. This dates all the way back to early man and our most basic survival instincts. Our brains have been conditioned to pay attention to negative stimuli because they may be a threat. These negative things register five times louder in our brains than positive messages do.

This correlates with intelligence. The more intelligent you are, the more prone to negative feelings you are. This is also because to survive in the past, the most intelligent person who was the most aware of danger would often survive to pass down their genes. These days we interact with so much negativity and encounter so much adversity that it is a conditioned response.

But think about this—just because the information is louder does not make it more valuable. It actually means that in order to quiet your mind, you have to work five times harder at putting those negative thoughts aside and replacing them with softer, more positive ones.

When an individual gets caught up in negative emotions and thoughts, it is the same as falling down a noisy rabbit hole. What matters most is that the individual is mindfully aware of being in such a dark and negative place so that they can employ strategies to transcend such negativity.

These noisy rabbit holes are places that are visited by a lot of people. You need to learn how to rise out of them and break through their limitations. Using solid strategies to counter these "negativity attacks," you will gain a life balance advantage.

---

39 Eliminating Negative Thinking, http://www.learnmindpower.com/using_mindpower/eliminating_negative_thinking/

Phase 2(b): A Drink of Toxic Kool-Aid

The second part of this second step is related to other people. Do not forget that because you have your own energy in the world, it is impacted by other people's energy all the time. Moods rub off on close family members. One negative person can set a fire that disrupts an entire household.

I like to call this "toxic Kool-Aid" because it is shared without anyone even realizing what has happened. This kind of limitation happens when you listen to someone else's negative thinking or feelings and then you absorb and internalize them.

Negative statements spoken by those closest to you, like your family members, authority figures, or close friends—or even strangers—can impact your personal energy. That is why that saying "messing with my vibe" has become so common.

It is the reason why when an angry person or a sad one steps into a happy group of friends, they usually become a "downer" impacting and, in essence, infecting others with their negative, louder energies. Toxic Kool-Aid for everyone!

What other people say can have a seriously damaging toxic impact on your emotional and mental state. If you listen to a negative person for too long, your thoughts become negative. The danger of this happening to you during this awakening process is very real.

When your trusted friends and family come to speak to you, they may do it from a caring, good place, but sweet Kool-Aid to the thirsty can be poison in disguise. It is essential to be mindful of the toxic Kool-Aid that is offered, and to protect yourself against these negative suggestions and emotions.

Keep in mind that when a positive, happy person enters a room, all negative people drain their energy. Negative energy is stronger and louder after all. It would take several happy people to placate and transform someone in a dark place into someone who is in a good mood. One-on-one interactions often transfer negative energy from one person to the next.

You have to keep your guard up and maintain emotional distance from these experiences, or the energy will jump to you. Then you will find yourself taking it out on someone else or on something else in your life.

Phase 3: Constant Motion: Your Personal Energy

The final step is to understand the concept of personal energy. Energy is the most valued resource for us as people. It animates our bodies, gives us motion, and brings our ideas to life. You could say that energy is the essence of us at a particular point in time.

Your happiness is directly connected to your ability to manage energy. The term "personal energy" can be defined through a number of parts of you that people scarcely understand or even acknowledge. How you manage these determines what you are able to do in life.

A sense of "aliveness," your feelings and emotions, your thoughts, memories, a sense of purpose of direction, and conscious belief are all part of your personal energy. You cannot see any of these things, yet you know they are there. Your personal energy, then, is integral to who you are and how you perceive the world.

Your energy[40] gives you motion, which is great. Unfortunately, modern man has not caught up with the demands of our modern lives just yet. In the old days, all we had to do was find food and shelter and protect each other from predators and invaders. These days, in one single day a person can perform as many as 100 different critically-important-for-survival tasks.

Your personal energy is supposed to be managed, but because of the demands on our time, the focus has completely shifted over to time management. Being "on the go" all day and always having something to do, somewhere to be, or someone to talk to can be extremely draining. Just look at how cell phones and the mobile revolution have reshaped humanity.

---

40 "Energy Management" Leads to Good Health, Positive Outlook, http://www.humankinetics. com/excerpts/excerpts/energy-management-leads-to-good-health-positive-outlook

Now you are constantly connected with 500 other people on multiple platforms, who can speak to you directly at any given time. This makes room for a lot of negativity coming at you from all sorts of places. Your personal energy is no longer being managed when you do not get time for yourself and your own wellbeing anymore.

Personal energy is renewable and sustainable if treated with care. People that focus on managing their energy are happier, healthier, and in touch with who they are as people. This is why high energy correlates with happiness and low energy correlates with sadness. Living in a perpetual state of low energy is downright dangerous for your wellbeing.

The Energy Spendthrift

I would go so far as to call the average dysfunctional person an energy spendthrift. This person spends all of their time tending to the needs of other people, and they ignore themselves. These individuals are often reflect the lowest energy and the unhappiest.

There is a good reason for this too. You cannot spend your energy on other people all the time and save none for yourself. How do you recharge? How do you build resilience against the negatives in the world? Without energy, you cannot do any of that.

Energy is a wonderfully fragile thing if you study it, as I have. It begins as nutritional intake and is transformed into kinetic energy in the body, which fuels our thoughts and movements. So if you do not have a healthy diet, you will never have enough energy. You kill your chance at wellbeing before you ever get to any of the other steps.

Consequently, when you go out to work and expend the energy that you have on work, on your loved ones, and on friends, it saps the rest away. Our overly busy lives have turned many of us into energy spendthrifts. We simply do not fully realize how our actions are causing us to be depressed, anxiety-ridden, and dissatisfied with life!

When you have a lot of energy and feel refreshed, I bet you, under normal circumstances, could take on a roomful of people at a party.

But if you arrive home after your boss has berated you, you are not going to feel like the "life of the party."

The bottom line is that your personal energy is not infinite; it is finite. Even *Harvard Business Review* has done studies on personal energy and how it needs to be better managed. They have found that when companies can help their staff manage their energy, productivity[41] improves far more than with time management.

Put another way—if you do not have the personal energy to avoid the "holes," you will keep falling into them. Motion breeds motion, and inactivity breeds inactivity. Be aware of the energy that you spend and the energy that you absorb because it impacts your entire person.

---

41 Tony Schwartz, Manage Your Energy, Not Your Time, https://hbr.org/2007/10/manage-your-energy-not-your-time

CHAPTER 6
STEPPING WISELY: THIS IS HOW YOU WAKE UP

"As a single footstep will not make a path on the earth,
so a single thought will not make a pathway in the mind.
To make a deep physical path, we walk again and again.
To make a deep mental path, we must think over and over
the kind of thoughts we wish to dominate our lives."
Henry David Thoreau

In order to learn how to step wisely, I want to introduce you to clear methods that you can use to change the way that you think so that spotting "holes" in your life becomes second nature. The more holes you spot, the more self-aware you will become. It is only once you have identified a problem that you can begin to work on correcting it.

This chapter is dedicated to you learning how to wake up from your sleepwalk. I want to expose you to nine easy steps that you can take to make "waking up" easier as you move through your average day. Remember that practice makes perfect!

The Self-Discovery Frontier

Did you ever love children's search books when you were younger? The ones where a fellow in red and white stripes would be placed on an impossibly busy page and you would have to find him? These Where's Waldo books perfectly explain what it is like seeking out mindfulness when it comes to your own thoughts and behaviors.

The first step you need to take to break free of your sleepwalk is to embrace this "Where's Waldo" mindset. Being observant and attentive about your habits and actions means looking at yourself under a microscope—not just how you are but who you are in the context of other people. You will be surprised at what you find!

This is the self-discovery[42] frontier that you have dedicated yourself to. You need to be curious about Waldo/Waldette (you!), where he/she is, and what he/she is getting involved in. Are you aware that your thoughts are based on a belief system and that this stream of consciousness determines who you are and who you will become?

Are you aware that the results of your actions—positive or negative—are all realizations that offer you valuable feedback? Being passionate about self-discovery is a commitment. Every day you need to seek out Waldo/ Waldette. This is the frontier you need to adventure into.

Step 1: Commit to self-discovery.

The Expert Within (You Know Yourself Best)

The second step in this process is to listen to the expert within you. That means noticing yourself, what you think, what you say, and how you interact with other people. You know yourself best! Now that you are committed to self-discovery, you have to begin a vast observation and listening process, whereby you try to determine what you want.

---

42   Theo J. Ellis, Why Smart People Commit to Self Improvement Everyday, http:// justbereal.co.uk/why-smart-people-commit-to-self-improvement-everyday/

For a long time your body, mind, emotions, and interpersonal and spiritual sides have been trying to tell you things that you have been ignoring. Perhaps you have become too attached to your life roles and have allowed the stress of them to drown out your inner voice.

Whether you are a father, a wife, a son, or a niece, sometimes you have to distance yourself from these definitions if you want clarity about yourself. After all, a single person is many things, and one single thing cannot define them completely.

Noticing yourself[43] means determining what your personal goals are and how these relate to the people, places, and things in your life. This will help you find your own path to happiness, or at least the beginning of that narrow road that you will have to walk down.

When you practice shifting your attention towards your spirit through self-observation, you can learn to "get out of your own way." This can be a handy tool in your arsenal when stressors are high and it seems as though you may step into a few dark holes again.

It is no secret that self-observation leads to enlightenment about who you are. So many people are on auto-pilot that they do not even realize the impact of their thoughts or actions. Take time to reflect on your thoughts and actions each day.

There is an inner voice inside you that you need to tap into because it speaks to you. Take note of what it is saying—is it helpful, or will it hinder you? Once you have learned to observe how you are, you can spot patterns of behavior. This will enable you to step outside of yourself when you have been upset or there is conflict in your life.

Step 2: Observe your thoughts and behaviors.

---

43   Terri Cole, How to Become the Observer and Liberate Yourself, http://www.positivelypositive.com/2014/03/14/how-to-become-the-observer-and-liberate-yourself/

The Only Existing Moment in Time

The third step that you need to learn in order to wake up from your eternal sleepwalk is to accept this present moment. When you live shrouded in darkness, you are in bondage to time and it controls you. This means that you are fearful of the past, worried about the future, and never in the present moment.

As a result, you sacrifice your "now" to overwhelming emotions that are neither constructive nor worthwhile. The past has happened, and it is gone. The future is uncertain and changes constantly. Worrying about either of these is a great way to drive yourself insane with fear because of a ticking clock.

The only existing moment in time is now. Allowing yourself to experience the present moment means living life to its fullest. Now is the best place to be because philosophically, it is the only real place where we exist.

Being present is made more powerful when we learn to add value to it. We find out how to respond to situations we are confronted with because we are aware of our own feelings. When you understand that no one can harm you emotionally unless you let them, it becomes a shield that helps you move forward in the present.

When experts[44] say that your life is determined by you, for you, it is true. The small changes that we make right now impact our tomorrows. Your today, in fact, is a product of what you did yesterday—think about that. If you are not happy with your "now," then you were not paying enough attention to your needs yesterday.

This present moment is about being mindful all the time. Even when you believe you are multitasking, you are not. People can only focus on one thing at a time. Simplify your now, and slow down your present. Take a breath, consider what you are investing your time and energy into, and if you would like to, change it.

---

44   Michael J. Formica, 5 Steps for Being Present, https://www.psychologytoday.com/blog/enlightened-living/201106/5-steps-being-present

Let go of residual feelings, especially if they are bad for you. Focus on making yourself feel happy right now, in the moment—and you know what? You will be happier. This is the only time that you will ever have. Learning to use it wisely is a skill.

Step 3: Be in the present moment.

Life Energy Management

Your fourth step after you have taken the first three will be to learn a valuable life skill. That skill is figuring out how to manage your life energy by practicing life balance. I cannot express how crucial this step is in the process, which is why I have dedicated much of this book to teaching you strategies on how you can achieve this.

Life energy management is more important than time management because it focuses on your needs and not the external needs of the world. When you dedicate yourself to life balance, you begin to analyze each part of who you are—your physical, mental, emotional, relational, and spiritual sides are all stripped bare.

There is energy to be found in each of these five areas of life balance, and because energy in the human system is multidimensional, managing it means learning some tough lessons along the way. There is a fundamental link between these sides of yourself, and if you misspend the energy you are given, you will never have enough to do what you need to do or be happy.

Even a small change in one dimension of energy[45] is enough to throw the other four into distress. Consider hunger, for example, one of my favorite analogies. Hunger is a deep physical need that impacts every part of you, which is why the need to eat is such an important thing for the body. It sends up warning flairs that our energy is running low.

---

45   Jean Kelley, Forget Time Management...Are You Managing Your Energy?, http://www. affluentmagazine.com/articles/article/664

To do this, your body will respond in different ways—you will feel physical distress, mentally you will not be able to stop thinking about food, and emotionally you will become irritable and will fall into a bad mood because you feel so low. This will send your interpersonal side into distress as you become frustrated with people you encounter.

Treating these people badly will upset your spiritual side, and all five sides of your energy will plummet into a bad place until you are able to locate and consume food. This energy management system is very telling. You have to watch out for internal and external stressors and how they impact your energy. You also need to make sure yours is in abundance.

Step 4: Manage your life energy with life balance.

The Long-Neglected Spirit

The fifth step on your path to awakening yourself involves the spirit that lies within you. Yes, you have a spirit, and it is a very active and important part of your life. Some people like to refer to the spirit as your "inner voice" or the part of you that cannot be seen: your soul.

As human beings, we consist of much, much more than simply hours of daily thoughts, beliefs, attitudes, and feelings. In our modern society, the spirit is repressed or made to be unimportant, but this is not how anyone should live. Some monks say that neglecting your spirit is the most certain way to never find inner peace or happiness.

Our Western culture has long neglected the spirit, instead replacing it with short-term material things that are used to fill that void. Instead of listening to our spirits, we buy fancy cars and bend over backwards to get that promotion at work. But your spirit can only be touched through silence, meditation, and other transcendent activities.

One example might be going out into nature and praying. Have you ever done this? The feeling of connection that you get is overwhelming and quite different to the dull sensations that you experience on a day-to-day basis. To awaken the spirit within you, you need to practice more of these moments of silent transcendence.

When you do, you will get in touch with your inner wisdom, and those deep hidden aspirations will come to light. They can only manifest once you have found them, but once you have, they will spring into action and create meaningful non-coincidences in your life.

Tending to the long-neglected spirit[46] means putting your ego aside to reduce your fight, flight, or protect mode. Hopefully, you will learn to nourish and feed your spirit so that it grows and guides you. Gratitude, innovation, helping others, and satisfaction all feed the spirit. Learn to feel and embrace love and to appreciate what you have in your life more often.

The spirit is what benefits most when you practice positive thinking and actions because then you become geared to feed your spirit all the time. This is the most direct path to happiness, and it can take a lifetime to perfect.

Step 5: Awaken and feed your spiritual side.

Attention: Free Today Only

The sixth step to awakening from your sleepwalk involves learning an essential life lesson. I have spoken about personal energy and how people can impact you. This works both ways! Your personal energy can impact other people too. By the time you reach this step, you should be focusing on that.

That is why you need to learn to offer your attention freely for the benefit of others. Wherever you go in life, you bring your

---

46 Angelica Rose, Awakening the Inner Spirit, http://www.awakening360.com/article/awakening-the-inner-spirit-angelica_rose#sthash.Eo6Jhgi6.dpbs

personal presence with you. That personal presence is made up of a number of things: your energy, care and concern, mindful attention, appreciation, and compassion.

What better way to use your personal presence than to bless others with it? Try to leave people in a better place than before they encountered you. That is the rule with this step. If you can do this, not only will you be feeding a spiritual need but you will also be acting in a way that aligns with positive energy and good forces, thereby attracting them to you.

Learning to offer your attention[47] freely is a real gift. For a stressed out friend, it can mean comfort when they really need it. For a lost family member, it can mean solid advice when they are in a bad space. However you choose to use it, begin to see people as more than their actions and behaviors.

Attention really is free, and it is one of the most valuable things in the world. Learning to give people your full attention is a skill that attracts others to you. You should be able to see people who need attention and make them feel comfortable by giving it to them. Attention is about taking the time to notice what people need.

Your personal presence can be a blessing to people who come across you. By engaging with people in a mindful, positive way, you will feel your social circles expanding, and people will naturally want to be around you more often. Just be careful of that toxic Kool-Aid scenario because that does not help you. You have to protect yourself too!

Step 6: Offer your attention freely.

---

47   M. Farouk Radwan, How to Use the Weapon of Attention to Attract People to You, http://www.2knowmyself.com/attention_and_attracting_people_to_you

Communication and Positive Influence

The seventh step on your path to becoming self-aware is to learn to communicate effectively so that you positively influence other people. Again, being a positive influence in the lives of others is great for the spirit inside you.

I have observed different professionals across multiple fields, and it has become clear that great communicators have one thing in common: they will successfully influence people in specific ways. Before you can effectively influence others, you must become a student of effective interpersonal communication.

Some people learn this naturally as they grow up in balanced social environments. Others who come from a lot of dysfunction need to learn it as adults. The meaning of your communication can always be measured by the response it elicits regardless of our initial intent. People act as mirrors, and it is your job to respond appropriately.

This can be a complex and multifaceted thing, which is why so few people are "power influencers" in the world. Your personal power is communicated by your energy levels, your thoughts, and your actions. By focusing these on a person or a group of people, you can learn to influence them in positive ways.

Communication[48] is built around socializing, relationships, consulting, alliance building, exchanging, stating, modeling, persuading, and many other key methods of strong influence transfer. If you are going to share your positive energy with others and influence them to be better, stronger, happier people, this will need to be practiced often.

Be an inspiring example of how someone can seize control of their destiny and reshape their lives. Make other people feel important, project confidence, and offer your attention to the people around you that genuinely need it. Let your spirit guide you, and you will see how rewarding sharing your personal space can be.

---

48   How Influence Works, http://www.theelementsofpower.com/index.cfm/how-influence-works/

Communication and positive influence are not about getting your way. They are about listening to others, helping them, and offering them validation and attention so that they can feel rewarded from a positive social interaction. Practice this skill, and you will never find yourself alone and without friends. Leave people feeling great, and they will always return.

> ### Step 7: Communicate with and positively influence others.

The Fulfillment Experience

The eighth step that you should take, once you have perfected the other seven, is to understand and practice the concept of fulfillment. True and lasting happiness comes directly from experiences that fulfill your heart and spirit.

If you reach back into moments of your life when you felt happy, I bet it was always when something significant was happening to someone close to you or when you had done something great for someone else. For an experience to be fulfilling, other people have to be involved; that is how we have been designed.

Unfortunately, people live with the delusion that happiness comes from moments of personal wealth, pleasure, or when that "soul mate" finally appears. This is simply not the case at all, because fulfillment is an ongoing recurrence in life.

Lasting happiness[49] comes from one's contributions, spiritual insights, and the expansion of our personal and collective consciousness. Life is all about the meaning you add to it, and without fulfillment, there is no meaning. Meaning at its depth is what generates happiness.

---

49   Deepak Chopra, Deepak Chopra: How To Recognize Life's Abundance, http://www.oprah.com/spirit/Deepak-Chopra-How-to-Feel-More-Fulfilled

In this step, you need to begin practicing the art of contentment and happiness by having fulfilling experiences. That means using self-awareness to put aside external stimuli to focus on your own experience of things and on creating fulfilling experiences for others.

Remember the last time you genuinely helped someone? Think back to a time when you did something that took time and effort and asked nothing in return. The work may have been hard, but amidst it, there was true happiness and fulfillment. Helping each other and sharing life's abundance is what we are all here to do.

There is a reason why people that volunteer at soup kitchens feel content with their lives, and that is because they actively practice sharing fulfilling experiences. You can do this in many ways in your own life to make you and your loved ones happy. The goal, as always, is to inspire generosity of spirit and to show others that good exists in the world.

Step 8: Gain fulfillment by helping others experience it.

Yes, Your Purpose Is Real...

Step nine, and the final step on your path to waking from your sleepwalk so that you can make it across the tightrope or so that you can dodge the holes along your path, involves your life purpose. As I was saying, in life, meaning is everything.

We yearn for meaning because we know it is something our spirits need to feel fulfilled. If you are going to reach a full-blown state of self-awareness, then you will uncover your life's purpose. It may have been hidden from you until now, crushed under the weight of your daily stress and busyness, always lingering but never fully realized.

Your purpose is real. Each of us has one, and to pursue it is to find happiness. One of the most effective ways of being happy is to discover your purpose then use it to help others have fulfilling experiences. This is how you convert who you are into how you can help others. After all, in the end, it is not about what you have but who you have helped.

We are truly happiest in life when we have come to realize how best to spend it. This maximizes our use of time, energy, and everything in between. It makes our mistakes worthwhile and our successes important. It gives us the meaning that we crave.

In the words of Howard Thurman, "There is something in every one of you that waits and listens for the sound of the genuine in yourself. It is the only true God you will ever have. And if you cannot hear it, you will all your life spend your days on the end of strings that someone else pulls."

It can take a lifetime[50] to uncover your life's purpose. With every step you take in that direction, new opportunities will guide you closer to where you are meant to be. Never dismiss that quiet voice inside you that wants to have a say in your life. This is who you are inside and is the truest version of yourself.

At the end of self-awareness, there is a realization of your life's purpose. This purpose needs to be used to help others so that you can be happy and generate positive experiences in people's lives. When you get older and you measure your life, do not measure it in wealth but in love and leadership—and who in the world you have raised above yourself.

Step 9: Uncover your life purpose.

---

50   Jeanine Byers, How to Uncover Your Life Purpose Even If You Have No Idea!, http://www.trans4mind.com/counterpoint/index-life-purpose/byers.shtml

PART III

THE LIFE BALANCE ADVANTAGE

CHAPTER 7
THRIVING WITH IMPERFECTION

"No person, no place, and no thing has any power over us, for 'we' are the only thinkers in our mind. When we create peace and harmony and balance in our minds, we will find it in our lives."

Louise L. Hay

We live in an unbalanced world where work is more important than children, time is more important than work, and spiritual fulfillment is at the very end of a long list of to-dos, if it even makes it onto the list. That is why in order to lead a happy, fulfilled existence, you have to learn how to thrive with imperfection in your life.

That means learning what life balance really is and how to make the most of it in your own life, according to your own personal needs. As you awaken from your long sleepwalk and become more self-aware, your needs will become more apparent. Before they begin to tax you, you should address them to achieve your ideal life balance.

The Imperfect World Explained

The world is far from perfect. Every day people bustle to and from work in order to earn money so that they can afford to live and attain the success[51] that they feel they deserve. The demands of success are great, and it takes nearly all of your time. Eventually, you are working more than you are living.

Sometimes you have to work simply to survive and not to live. There are many traps in the world, debt being one of them, and it keeps a lot of people struggling for air. Life is a multifaceted experience, and leading a balanced life can be an enormous challenge.

There is only a finite amount of time and energy in your average day that you have to spend. What you choose to spend it on has largely been driven by your external needs until now. From this moment on, you need to consider your internal needs before your external needs.

Have you ever wondered why there is never enough time to do everything that you want to do in your life? Why you always seem drained and unable to function at your peak? There are real reasons for this, and they have to do with the way that you choose to live.

Doing more and more and more is not the answer. This simply creates compression, which causes a rise in pressure, and eventually, you explode from the effort. It is not about time either but about leading a balanced life. Only balance can restore the power that you have lost through mismanaged time and energy placement.

Your Inner Longing: Higher Levels

Your life has been very externally driven until now. You have been pursuing wealth, success, fame, and fortune—and it has done nothing but make you miserable. Life by its very nature is imperfect and unbalanced.

Due to this, difficulties will arise for you from ordinary daily events, changing circumstances, and the trance nature of conditioned

---

51   Living a Balanced Life in an Unbalanced World, http://advancedlifeskills.com/blog/seeking-balance-in-an-unbalanced-world/

existence. These moments that we have to endure are only temporary. They are caused by change and are meant to unsettle you, as if to jar you awake from the sleep that you have been in.

In order to transcend the negative effects that can arise out of your subjective interpretations of the world and of adverse experiences in your life, you need to develop a higher level of self-control. It is this self-control that will help you break out of your current mindset.

This is the inner longing that you need to move towards to gain higher levels of self-awareness and personal growth. It will be reflected in the commitment that we develop towards our own personal wellness and happiness.

I love the saying "you should put legs on your longings" because it fits in so nicely with our sleepwalking analogy. When your eyes are closed, you have little self-control. You cannot see what you eat, where you are going, what you look like, or how you appear to other people. You are as blind as you can be.

But when you open your eyes, you put legs on your longing for self-control. You realize what you have been eating, where you should be going, what you look like, and how you appear to other people.

You become a transparent and malleable person who is self-aware and ready to change for the better. Then it becomes a matter of disciplining yourself and embracing that change. Your inner longing for balance has been trying to get your attention for some time now.

To achieve it, you need to increase your levels of self-discipline. Unfortunately, nothing worth having in this life comes easily. You will need to walk along many skinny tightropes to achieve some great destinations, but it is very possible when you have inner balance.

The Concept of Personal Wellness

Personal wellness is where self-awareness leads you. Once you become aware of yourself as a living, breathing human being with a set of needs, you have to find a way to fulfill them. I am talking, of course, about your internal needs—the ones that make you happy and fulfilled—not merely the external trappings of a materialistic world.

Personal wellness relates directly to energy management. You need to manage the five areas of energy in your life in order to achieve peak performance, ultimate health, and a life balance that suits you. These key areas are physical, emotional, mental, interpersonal, and spiritual. They govern how you feel and behave and what your attitude might be.

Energy is the fundamental factor in the achievement of high performance living, or you "living the best life" you can live. Every thought, feeling, and human interaction has an energy consequence. It is our most valuable resource, and people spend it frivolously every day!

But personal wellness means learning how to manage your energy stores and how to spend them on the right areas in your life so that you can achieve balance and have the fortitude to fight back against obstacles when they arise.

To have energy every day for the things that matter, you need to tend to your five energy areas. If they are being neglected, you will find yourself experiencing negative side effects of energy drain.

When, for example, you do not eat breakfast and also skip lunch, by the time you get to dinner time, your body is super low on physical energy and cannot muster up enough of the other energies to compensate. You become ratty, unfocused, and irritable as a result.

Energy[52] in the human system is multidimensional. A dynamic relationship exists between physical, emotional, mental, interpersonal, and physical energies. As a LAW, changes in any one dimension of energy will impact or affect all energy dimensions.

Our most favorable energy condition to be in as human beings is this:

---

52 Kim Farbota, 5 Steps to Maximize Efficiency by Managing Your Energy, Not Your Time, http://www.huffingtonpost.com/kim-farbota/success-and-motivation_b_5367183. html

- Physically energized
- Emotionally centered
- Interpersonally connected
- Mentally focused
- Spiritually aligned

Peak performance in all aspects means optimizing performance through energy balance. This is done by learning how to balance each of your five energy dimensions.

Drains on Your Energy Stores

The biggest part of learning how to manage your energy is learning how to recognize when things start draining your energy and it becomes lost. To be able to stop to restore one of your energy dimensions because you are self-aware enough to do so is a gift.

Your energy becomes lost[53] when:

- You are physiologically depleted.
- You are experiencing negative emotions.
- Your mental awareness is narrow and not present-moment focused.
- Your interpersonal connections to teammates, family, and significant others become unconstructive.
- Your spiritual alignment fails to be value-driven, and you become vainly self-absorbed.

In order to maintain your energy stores, you need to understand these areas of wellness:

- *Physical wellness:* Your body is essentially ephemeral and limited and should be respected. Your human body deteriorates,

---

53   Marc Chernoff, 10 Toxic Habits That Drain Your Energy, http://www.marcandangel. com/2014/08/24/10-toxic-habits-that-drain-your-energy/

so you need to invest your time and energy into maintaining this spiritual vessel. Monitoring your proper nutrition and appropriate levels of activity and allowing for daily rest are absolutely essential.

- *Emotional wellness:* Your feelings vacillate from moment to moment. Being able to identify and differentiate from your emotions and articulate them appropriately to other people is essential to your state of wellbeing.

- *Mental wellness:* Your mind changes like the weather; thinking is unpredictable and changeable. But we are not simply the sum of our thoughts. The mind is fickle, so you should not rely on it. Remaining mindful and investing in a form of mental discipline like meditation is a must. Your will and intention directs your mind and controls the way that you think, speak, and behave. Your intentions establish your life priorities and inevitably create your destiny.

- *Interpersonal and familial wellness:* The ability for you to communicate effectively with other people, especially family and loved ones, is essential to long-lasting health and wellness.

- *Spiritual wellness:* A truly spiritual and meaningful life is discovered in our ability to contribute to others and the world around us. Vocational and educational satisfaction is important in life as long as you live in a way that honors your spiritual connectedness. Many arrive later in life to discover that they are very successful yet the ladder had been leaning on the wrong wall the entire time.

These are the main areas of concern if you want to attain personal wellness and achieve life balance in your lifetime.

The Life Balance Assessment

In order to achieve life balance, you need to be able to assess yourself according to the five main energy areas that keep you performing well as a human being. Healthcare costs have skyrocketed these days, have you noticed?

The families that cannot receive much-needed healthcare are destined to live a very compromised existence, if they survive. People need much more proactive preventative measures instead of an analgesic approach, which does nothing but dampen their troubled emotions. People need to assume more responsibility for their overall wellbeing.

I believe that as human beings, we all need to aggressively approach life balance[54] in our lives so that we can live, not only survive. Removing self-medication tendencies is a great start to this. A new life balance approach will empower others to proactively seek spiritual and emotional remedies as a first line of defense.

Sufferers that actively seek energy-based solutions, not just conventional treatments, will benefit the most from this practice. Life balancing practices like these will shift the individual's self-defeating beliefs and fears rather than suppress them with prescription drugs.

One of the biggest problems in the world is that 65% of people have never learned healthy stress reduction techniques, and life is extremely stressful! This is especially true of modern life, where you are expected to be on the go all the time like a machine.

You need to wake up to the fact that your limited awareness could be costing you your physical health, emotional and mental stability, healthy relationships, and spiritual alignment. Without these things, we are nothing—less than people and barely human.

Individuals are not consciously programmed; they are conditioned to avoid discomfort by covering up their life's pain. Many of my clients failed to realize that self-medicating patterns were destructive, sedating, and distracting them from the uncomfortable effects of stress.

To make matters even worse, there are villains and enemies that would prefer you to stay asleep on the couch and out of touch with

---

54   A Balanced Life, http://www.mommd.com/canyouhaveitall.shtml

who you are. They do not want you to notice that these conditioned realities are harming you. But make no mistake, there is adversity in this world, and it is pushing against you for many basic reasons.

Adversity Is a Great Teacher

It is true, there are villains in this world that are out to get you. But they do not wear black masks and carry ray guns. They do not come with an army of minions to do their bidding. These villains are hidden in plain sight all around us, bouncing off each other, continually passing negative energy from one area to the next in cycles.

It comes from places like the media and advertisers who thrive on fear and quick fixes, from loved ones that suggest you self-medicate to alleviate these uncomfortable feelings that you have been having about your life, and, naturally, from yourself—you get in your own way a lot. The real enemy in all of these instances is non-reality, big business, and misinformation.

Media outlets pump our minds full of options to self-medicate the hardships of life away. Mental health issues are real, granted, and they do sometimes require medications. But businesses have vested interests in persuading people that they have a mental illness. It could be argued that the rates of mental illness have remained the same for years.

The only thing that has changed is that we allowed drug companies to openly persuade people that they have mental instability. It is quite difficult these days to visit your doctor without getting a prescription for some or other medication. The psychiatric industry grosses $150,000 every minute.

Pharmaceutical sales are a $271 billion dollar industry. There are 700,000 adverse side effects due to medications that happen each year, with 42,000 deaths annually. In 2009, $4.5 billion[55] in

---

55   Bo Wang, The Role of Direct-to-Consumer Pharmaceutical Advertising in Patient Consumerism, http://journalofethics.ama-assn.org/2013/11/pfor1-1311.html

pharmaceutical advertising was spent, and along with that, some 1,000,000 kids were diagnosed with bi-polar disorder—which is more common than autism and diabetes combined. Why is that?

There are many dark enemies that you need to watch out for that negatively impact your life energy. This list is seemingly endless; drugs, alcohol, food, sex, unhealthy relationships, money, shopping, gambling, social media and obsessive technology, negative thinking, self-doubt, procrastination, and resentment are all trying to thwart us.

At any time in your life, one or many of these things can disrupt or influence your energy in a negative way, resulting in a total shift of your performance and a retreat back into slumber. Being self-aware means understanding these threats and taking them for what they are.

The Optimal Energy Blend

The formula for the perfect amount of energy has already been given to us, but attaining it in our daily lives is the ongoing challenge. Because each day is packed with its own points of adversity and its own tests, you have to be mindful throughout your day.

This is the basis for total self-awareness—the ability to detect when something negative has stepped into your personal space and is messing with your energy. Once detected, you can counter this adversity by practicing something that will rebalance your energy in a positive way. Think of us as signals in a television; sometimes we go snowy and need to be adjusted for a clear picture of the world to come back into focus.

- Focus on becoming physically energized each and every day. This means taking a hard look at the fuel that you put into your body and how it impacts you. Take food that nourishes[56] and renews you into consideration even if you are not a big fan yet. Eat well, and eat for nutrition. Focus on getting enough movement and motion into your day with the right kind of exercise, and take time to meditate to center yourself.

- Focus on becoming emotionally centered.[57] When you are emotionally balanced, you can be resilient when people around you break down, and you are not so easily sucked into negative mindsets nor are triggered to experience negative emotions by other people. With a positive balance comes the ability to think clearly, even through times of great emotional stress, which is a huge asset.

- Focus on becoming interpersonally connected. Everyone in the world needs people that they can trust, care for, rely on, and love. It gives us a reason for existing, and it helps us find our place in the world. When you have a close network of friends and family, you are taking care of your social energy. We need this energy to feel connected to each other and validated by each other.

- Focus on becoming mentally focused. Real mental focus and clarity comes with great wisdom and the understanding that while many things can impact your mindset, only you can control it. Avoiding distractions, getting down to business, and working in your best interest is what this type of energy wants to do. Being mentally tough will keep you thinking independently and concentrating on your own wellbeing.

- Focus on becoming spiritually aligned. The spirit is something we have all but forgotten in modern times. No, not mindlessly attending church, temple, or mosque or ascribing to a religion but being in touch with your spirit—what fulfills you, what drives you, and what keeps you going. Your spirit is at the core of who you are, and it wants to be acknowledged.

---

57   Emotionally Centred: Passion Power & Rationalization Ruin, http://www.themichaelteaching.com/sessions/no-fault-communication/passions-rationalizations/

An Introduction to You

You are the balance that makes up your five different energy sources. When one is out of balance, the rest become impacted. If you do not believe me, here are two different scenarios so that you can see who the "real you" is behind the scenes.

A man wakes up, has a full breakfast, and is in a good mood. He goes to work and sits through a meeting, where his boss publically humiliates him in front of the team. For the rest of the day, his emotions are shot, which impacts his ability to perform at work. He skips lunch because he is so distracted, and when he gets home, he has a fight with his wife.

In this scenario, the man's emotional wellbeing is attacked, which impacts his mental wellbeing, his physical wellbeing, and eventually his interpersonal wellbeing. Like dominoes, they each fall because he could not recognize the real impact that the negative transference of emotional energy from his boss had on his personal wellbeing.

A woman wakes up, does not eat breakfast, and goes to work. She is very nervous about a presentation that she has to give, but it goes off well. Afterwards her colleague comes up to her and tells her what a great job she did on her presentation, and they have lunch together. The woman picks up some dinner on the way home and is pleased to see her family when she gets there.

In this scenario, the woman wakes up and starts her day out badly by offsetting her physical energy; she is also impacted by negative emotional stress due to her job. But this all changes when she is given positive interpersonal connection by a colleague. She is able to eat healthy to replenish her lost energy, and her mood improves around her family as a result.

One scenario is good, the other is bad—and they are both the result of different energy interactions that influence their personal wellbeing during the average day. You might encounter a nasty boss or a positive friend, but being able to identify what is impacting you is key. Then you can take action to fix it so that you can perform at your best.

You are the summation of many things, but your energy determines how your day goes, what you feel, how quickly you can recover from adversity, and ultimately your overall health. Learn to control your energy and take care of it, and you will master self-awareness.

CHAPTER 8
THE DOMAINS YOU NEED TO BALANCE

*"God gives every bird its food but He does not
throw it into its nest."*
J.G. Holland

Gaining the life balance advantage is about learning how you can go about rebalancing yourself when your specific energy areas are thrown out of whack. To do this, you must have a greater understanding of each domain and how it serves you as a human being.

These domains need to be balanced in the long term and on a short-term basis as you move through your average day. It is the small choices that we make daily that compound into our energy levels, affecting how we feel and how we respond to life.

My Story: The Physical Domain

The physical domain is involved with the choice that you have to create energy and vibrancy in life. If you want to be present, you have to be there on purpose. That means zooming your focus in on something to pay full attention to what is in front of you.

Keep your mind free from clutter, and do not focus on the small stuff. You can choose to focus on things you can control and get excited about them. When was the last time you simply decided to be happy or enthusiastic about something? How excited are you right now?

Most Americans are overweight because of their eating choices. We live in a "mega plate" society, let's face it. If everyone ate a little less at the table or when out, they would be much healthier and more likely to live with the positive energy that our bodies deserves.

If you master your eating choices, you master your metabolism and lose weight. If you want more energy, then talk to your doctor or nutritionist about reducing the amount of food that you eat per meal and focus on your meal choices to enhance your metabolism.

The physical domain[58] is also governed by how healthy you are, meaning that you need to factor exercise and rest into your daily regimen. Without movement and motion, your body will become tight and inflexible as well as prone to injury. Failure to ensure for adequate sleep and rest most certainly will negatively impact the quality of your life. Gaining weight and becoming inactive will unquestionably make it difficult to perform basic tasks. Make your life easier by exercising and taking time to rest daily!

An Intro to Physical Wellness

Physical wellness is all about mastering the three steps that allow you to have control over the physical domain. If you can master these steps, you can regain control over your physical energy.

---

58   Leo Widrich, The 4 Elements of Physical Energy and How to Master Them, https://blog.bufferapp.com/the-4-elements-of-physical-energy-on-how-to-master-them

There are three steps to mastering the physical domain:

Step 1: Choose live foods. Consider how much of your diet consists of fresh greens, vegetables, and fruit. Now consider how acidic or alkaline your current diet might be. Most Americans barely consume any greens, fruit, or vegetables at all in their diets.

They eat more meat and grain ("dead" foods) than any of these "live" foods. Water-rich live foods are great for your health and energy levels. They lower your blood's acidity level, detoxify your body, and boost your immune system.

Step 2: Physical movement. There is a very good reason why most people do not exercise consistently or intensely enough to improve their overall health and their waning energy levels. Many of them have accepted that they can only lead a "half-life" at a greatly reduced level of energy because they have no idea what they are missing out on.

Many of these individuals have never been trained to understand which exercises work best with their unique physical profile and why. They choose to limp around like zombies because their energy reserves are so low!

The bottom line is that if you want physical energy, you need to move! Dedicate at least three to five times a week to some intensive physical workout that will get your body moving. Dance, swim, run, do yoga—pick a type of movement, and make it work for you.

Step 3: Take time to relax. The other side of regular physical movement is taking time for relaxation. Just like muscles need time to grow larger after a heavy workout, your body needs time each day to relax and restore itself. The fastest way to boost your energy levels consistently is to find a balance between healthy eating, healthy movement, and healthy rest.

How energetic do you feel? If you are lacking in energy, then something is wrong! You need to eat better and exercise more. Fuel your body with the right stuff, and move it around regularly for an overall energy level that will keep you going all day long.

My Story: The Emotional Domain

People are highly emotional beings; there is no doubt about that. Sometimes it can feel as though we are chained to our feelings. This only becomes a problem when these emotional states become negative and un-resourceful.

This is when we can feel held hostage by our emotions in one way or another. While some people are confined and constrained by their fear of intense emotions—like inadequacy, sadness, hurt, and rejection—emotions can become like landmines. Then these individuals are forced to tiptoe through life trying to avoid these feelings.

Still others can never express their true emotions, like fear and doubt, because it helps them keep from ever taking a risky action. As emotional hostages, they are locked in a kind of paralysis. There are more people who are like victims to repetitive kidnapping by their emotions. Quite suddenly, emotion will strike them and distract them from the job at hand.

To relieve bad emotions and reach a pleasurable state, some people become slaves to addiction. Illicit drugs, alcohol, over the counter medications, nicotine, caffeine, and sugar are all substances that alter your mood. People that rely on addictions are making an effort to change or to reach these emotional states by choices that will ultimately complicate their lives.

Choice and control, in effect, are traded for the addiction. Many people pay a physiological price for enduring long periods of chronic emotion—sustained worry, fear, humiliation, hopelessness, anger, inadequacy, depression, and helplessness—and these can cause major stress increases leading to degenerative illness.

Things like gastrointestinal problems, high blood pressure,[59]

---

59 Mind/Body Connection: How Your Emotions Affect Your Health, http://familydoctor. org/familydoctor/en/prevention-wellness/emotional-wellbeing/mental-health/mind-body-connection-how-your-emotions-affect-your-health.html

heart disease, chronic fatigue syndrome, and diabetes are just a few. Emotions impact our lives so heavily, and yet most people lack any insight or choice in the matter. Their feelings run rampant through their lives.

Some emotions arrive like the weather and are unpredictable. Pleasant emotions surprise and delight, but they are short lived. There is a secret about emotional regulation that you should learn: when you exercise choice in your emotional expression, you develop the ability to respond to a wider range of emotions.

These people do not experience debilitation from their emotions, and if they do experience negative emotions, they do not dwell on them. They also respond to emotions, pleasant and unpleasant, with meaningful communication on how to make their lives better rather than chalk them up to attacks on them by a hostile environment.

An Intro to Emotional Wellness

Emotional wellness begins with awareness, as emotions are valuable information that your body receives telling you something of critical importance. Regardless of the pain or pleasure that ensues, this information must be weighed and judged for a response.

There are four basic competencies that you need to overcome your emotional state:

1. *The ability to respond to life's situations with emotions that are appropriate and useful.* Emotional regulation is therefore critically important as a feedback mechanism in life. If someone cracks a joke, you should laugh. If someone tells you a sad story, you should empathize. You should not feel like they are making fun of you or burst out into tears because you cannot regulate what you are feeling.

2. *The ability to choose how to express[60] your emotions.* As you

---

60 Guy Winch, Ph.D., 5 Habits That Will Improve Your Emotional Wellness, http://www. huffingtonpost.com/guy-winch-phd/emotional-wellness-tips_b_3809750.html

experience an emotion, it comes on like a wave of sensation. Then your physical body chooses how to express it. That is why when you are happy, you can laugh, smile, cheer, cry, or sob. It is why when you are really sad, you can laugh, shout, get angry, or cry all day. The choice is yours.

3. *The ability to utilize unpleasant emotions to generate useful behaviors and pleasant emotions.* A person that can, for example, take criticism constructively can, instead of taking it personally and breaking down in sobs, integrate the feedback they received and improve. The next round of feedback will be much more positive because of this—no need for an emotional breakdown.

4. *The ability to prevent yourself from experiencing certain overwhelming and immobilizing emotions.* When a person can emotionally distance themselves from a situation and not take things personally because they understand that it has more to do with the other individual's feelings and not their own, this becomes a superpower. A screaming boss will be rendered ineffective because you will not give them the rise out of you that they want.

The path to emotional wellness[61] is about gaining awareness of your thoughts and feelings, learning to utilize a positive attitude, learning how to seek out and express yourself emotionally in an appropriate way, and figuring out how to accept your mistakes and learn from them. If you can master these, you will become a master at emotional wellness.

My Story: The Mental Domain

Your mental domain is perhaps the most powerful and troubling of all of your personal domains, and it consistently impacts your health

---

61   Emotional Wellness, http://wellness.ucr.edu/emotional_wellness.html

and wellness. You have heard stories about great people using mental strength and stamina to overcome enormous odds and change the world based only on their mental clarity, will, and determination.

The mind is a powerful place, and it can work either for or against you in life. Sometimes mental clutter from a very busy life can overwhelm you, and keeping yourself going can feel like a process of spinning different plates and catching the ones that fall.

The mind sacrifices what it wants to do in order to do what needs to be done. The more tasks we are given in a day, the busier the mind gets. A modern schedule is a terrifying thing. Then there is the way that your mind is wired.

Sometimes you have learned a negative way to think and suffer with a victim mentality. Because of this, you perceive the world as a hostile place, where everything good happens to other people while you get dumped on.

But what is the difference between a happy person and a victim? Only perception, and that is governed by the mind. When you become self-aware, you begin to understand how you think, and you can critically evaluate your own thought processes to determine whether they are healthy or not.

If you are going to become a master of the mental domain, you need to focus on gaining mental clarity, strength, and will. Mental resilience, as it is called, is a huge precursor to success in life. This is not because is endows you with any special talents but because it gives you an iron will, and scientists[62] have determined that this is more important than intelligence.

Perseverance and passion straight from your mental domain will help you achieve the goals that you set for yourself in life. Right now, you may be like so many others—crippled by constantly flowing negative thoughts and an internal dialogue that clutters your life.

---

62   James Clear, The Science of Developing Mental Toughness in Your Health, Work, and Life, http://jamesclear.com/mental-toughness

The only way to break free of this stranglehold on your mind is to learn how to master it. Thoughts are living things, and they impact your personal wellness. Your mind needs to be rewired to be on your side so that you can thrive in life.

An Intro to Mental Wellness

To attain a state of psychological wellbeing, you need to make sure that the rest of your core needs are being met. This begins with what your mind needs. Developing mental toughness[63] and clarity and decluttering your thought processes is all part of the fun.

- The only person that needs to approve of who you are is you. Self-acceptance is key to mental clarity and a must-have for psychological wellness. Do not let other people define you; you were born special, and being different is perfectly okay. Often it is the different among us that influence the world the most.

- Always respect other people and yourself. This begins with self-love. You cannot love other people properly if you hate yourself and who you are. Respect is critical to the mind, and when you do not respect yourself, it can be a nightmare. Focus on learning to love yourself and getting what you want out of life.

- Do not indulge in negative toxic Kool-Aid. People will constantly try to dump their problems on you. And when your mind cannot solve their problems for them, it can become a very dangerous and unhealthy cycle of worry and despair. Accept that you can only do so much, and distance yourself from the negative chatter coming your way. This will help you maintain mental strength for more important things.

- Mistakes are okay, and they are learning opportunities. Always open yourself up to learning. The mind wants to learn and

---

63 Amy Morin, 5 Powerful Exercises to Increase Your Mental Strength, http://www.forbes.com/sites/groupthink/2013/12/03/5-powerful-exercises-to-increase-your-mental-strength/

evolve, but you have to guide it. If you focus on negative things, it will learn and evolve into those areas. If you focus on positive, uplifting things, it will learn and evolve there. Stay teachable!

- Meditation greatly decreases your stress and improves your happiness. To declutter your mind and give it time to reflect and process things, few things are better than daily meditation. Just 20 minutes of meditative practice can be enough to make you feel refreshed and to recharge the batteries in your mind. The research has shown for quite a long time that particular techniques, like Transcendental Meditation, can reduce cardiac output, normalize blood pressure, and increase intelligence and self-confidence while decreasing anxiety and depression. Have you ever wondered why we fail to teach this in grammar school?

- Limits begin when vision ends. Once a limiting thought is allowed into your consciousness and into the real world, these limitations shut down any positive expectations you might wish to have. Remind yourself to expand your internal vision of what is possible so that you can manifest your true potential.

- Remember that what you believe is your reality. Belief is a powerful tool for making your life successful. Learn how to harness belief for mental clarity and strength.

My Story: The Interpersonal Domain

Interpersonal wellness, or social wellness as it is more commonly called, is the domain that governs how you interact and behave around other people. Your ability to relate to and connect with other people in the world says a lot about who you are.

Gaining the ability to establish and maintain positive relationships with friends and family contributes to your social wellness. The ultimate quest in life is to develop relationships that are reciprocal, compassionate, and supportive.

If you want to master the art of creating these connections, then there are two foundational beliefs that are incredibly important to develop in yourself.

The first is to pay attention to the meaning of your communication and the response that it gets from others. The intent of your communication with others is not what matters; it is their interpretation of what you said to them and what meaning they assigned to the words or actions that matter. If the listener responds to your words with anger—regardless of your intentions—something has gone wrong.

You then need to take responsibility for how the other person interpreted your communication. Clarify your intended meaning with an attitude of acceptance. If what you have been doing does not elicit the responses you want, do something different!

Secondly, ultimate control is given to the person who has the most flexibility in communication. The person who demonstrates the most flexible behavior will always be the one in control. The ability to change your approach to communication, your attitude, and your feelings is a common characteristic of a respected leader.

In order to be in control of your communication, you must first be in control[64] of yourself. Control over both your thoughts and emotions is critical, along with control over your external world—your behaviors and actions.

You must decide in your relationships to consistently demonstrate inner and outer flexibility, like a tree whose branches will bend in the wind to avoid breaking. Bending requires that you have total conscious awareness and command over your internal state of being.

Control of your internal processes is the key to all viable behavioral change. This kind of "state" management is always the difference between success and failure with human interactions. Master yourself, and you will master interpersonal challenges.

---

64 Will Gemma, List of Interpersonal Skills: 10 Must-Have Attributes, https://blog.udemy.com/list-of-interpersonal-skills/

An Intro to Interpersonal Wellness

You can have all the success in the world, but if you are unable to manage your internal state, then you have nothing. If you can manage yourself, your mental wellness, and your emotional concerns, then you have broken down most limitations in life.

Remember that the quality of your life is equal to the quality of your ability to manage your state. You do this by moving your body (exercising) and changing what and how you focus on your internal processes (thoughts and feelings).

Interpersonal wellness is about maintaining rewarding, positive relationships with people. When your friends and family have a positive influence on your life, doors will open for you. This is because they positively impact your physical and mental health.

Recent scientific evidence[65] has shown that the need for friends in our lives is not optional at all but mandatory. Without friends, we simply do not function as whole people. Things like social isolation can be as bad for you as smoking cigarettes.

Having an active social life means different things to different people. Some people love to move in large crowds, and others only have one or two close friends. Seeing friends on a regular basis helps you keep in touch with the world and with who you are.

People have the most enormous influence over who we are and how we think, even though we do not consider this often enough. If you surround yourself with negative people, then you are far more likely to be negative yourself. The same can be said about positive people; this is why many successful people move in the same circles.

Human beings[66] are social creatures; we have a pack mentality, and we choose where and who we spend our time on. "Belonging" is a critical aspect of this as it helps you define who you are in the

---

65   What Social Wellness Is, https://socialwellness.wordpress.com/what-social-wellness-is/

66   The Importance of Social Wellness, http://movetowardwellness.com/what-is-wellness/social-wellness

world. To improve your own levels of social wellness, you will need to step outside of your comfort zone.

You need to recognize the need for recreation and how important it is to spend time with friends and family. Then you need to pursue activities and people that nurture your needs. Participation in different things, with different people, helps teach you life lessons and accelerates your rate of learning.

CHAPTER 9
A SPIRITUAL SENSE OF THINGS

"So be sure when you step. Step with care and great tact. And remember that life's a great balancing act! And will you succeed? Yes you will, indeed. Ninety eight and three-quarters percent guaranteed. Kid, you'll move mountains!"

Dr. Seuss

At the core of every human being on the planet lies a spirit. Yet our spiritual sides are often suppressed, ridiculed, and ignored because of modern sentiment and belief systems. The spiritual domain is perhaps the most important of all of them.

While in previous years spirituality has been defined through religion, it is being increasingly accepted that "the spirit" is not just a mental illusion or an institution but rather a real phenomenon that takes place inside each and every human being in the world.

My Story: The Spiritual Domain

Like many people around me, I once became seduced by the belief that success and happiness came with material and financial gain. I did not have many role models around me who spoke of spiritual benefits, and I found myself trying to uncover spiritual truths on my own. This was something I had to do for myself.

It was difficult considering that I had spent such a large amount of time fixed on the regrets of my past and the worries over my future. I used to see all the negativity of the days ahead and despair. Without a spiritual kindred to guide me in my early years, I found myself completely alienated from any family members who believed that something larger than "the self" existed within me. But it did.

Spirituality can mean many different things, but mainly it refers to approaches to discovering, experiencing, and living out the implications of an authentic human life. Your spirit transcends the material and mechanical world.

Spiritual wellness[67] is concerned with values and beliefs that provide us with purpose in our lives. It leads you to strive for a state of harmony with yourself and others and to balance your inner needs with the rest of your external world.

It is better to think about life's true meaning with an open mind than to be close-minded and intolerant of others. It is also better to live each day in a way that is consistent with your values and beliefs; otherwise you end up betraying your true self.

The Serious Nature of the Unfulfilled Spirit

People often have dreams that they feel compelled to follow in their lives. It is almost as if a magnetic force pulls them towards a destiny. If only they could find their way. When you feel pulled towards something but it seems unachievable, your spirit despairs.

---

67 Spiritual Wellness, http://wellness.ucr.edu/spiritual_wellness.html

An unfulfilled spirit[68] is a dangerous thing. We were all put here in this world to walk along our own unique spiritual journey. When we are unable to do that, we become extremely unhappy. Spiritual longing, like any sort of desire, can cause serious distress and can prove to be a massive obstacle on your road to balance.

Unfulfillment can be the key that unlocks a door to a lot of negative behaviors. To fill that void of longing, people will do just about anything. They fill it with material possessions, money, power, mind-altering substances, and people. Their life becomes about distraction from that longing.

Our bodies are containers for our souls or spirits. This is the essence of who we are and what we want from the world. You can never quiet a restless spirit. True happiness can only be achieved once you acknowledge that your spirit wants to guide you to where you are supposed to be in this life.

As you become more self-aware, your spirit begins to awaken again. Just like your heart longs[69] for love, your spirit longs for purpose and balance. The connection that we have to our spirit creates a feedback mechanism that transmits knowledge, love, light, and comfort to us—things that we need to grow and thrive as people.

If you have an unfulfilled spirit, it becomes impossible to be happy. You could be the richest man on earth and feel nothing but hopelessness. We are all made to walk our own paths, and your spirit is meant to help you find yours in your lifetime. The only way to get rid of that spiritual longing is to embrace it and try to discover what your true purpose is.

The Equality of Five Principle

There is great wisdom imparted on us by our spiritual longings. We should all be fully aware of what makes us happy and what does

68 Spiritual Longing and the Path of Forgiveness, http://www.worldblessings.com/spiritual-longing.html
69 Swami Krishnananda, Living a Spiritual Life, http://www.swami-krishnananda.org/spiritual.life/spiritual_09.html

not. We receive these learnings in the form of feedback through our experiences as people.

To become a more spiritual person, you need to respect all five of your domains and treat them as sacred—because they are. The Equality of Five Principle, as I like to call it, pertains to each of your personal wellness domains.

1. *Your physical domain:* Respect yourself enough to eat healthily, get fit, and afford yourself time to relax. You will be able to get in touch with your spiritual side a lot easier when you are in great shape. Your body is your temple!

2. *Your mental domain:* Respect your mind enough to understand how it works, and how you can change it to work in your best interests. When your mind is clear from clutter and stress, getting in touch with your spiritual side is easy.

3. *Your emotional domain:* Respect yourself enough to know what you are feeling and why. Use your awareness to control your emotions in a way that benefits you. When you master your emotions, you can connect with your spiritual side.

4. *Your interpersonal domain:* Respect your social needs enough to foster strong relationships with the people closest to you. They will teach you things about yourself and help you find your true path in life.

5. *Your spiritual side:* When your spiritual side is being acknowledged, you are guided through your daily decisions with your true path in mind. When you achieve equality throughout all of your domains, your spiritual side will have what it needs to engage and guide you to where you need to be.

The Equality of Five Principle should be kept in mind as you develop more self-awareness and begin to be pulled towards different things in your life. The better in tune you are with your other four domains, the clearer the pull will be from your spiritual domain.

Strategies for Reviving Your Spirituality

Research has shown us that people with a sense of spirituality are likely to experience greater happiness and wellbeing in life. It can provide you with a sense of meaning, vitality, and a sense of connectedness to others and to something "bigger" beyond your daily life.

There are many strategies[70] that can help you get back in touch with your spiritual side. I suggest doing it by reconnecting with specific feelings and practices in your life.

1. *Practice gratitude.* Nothing connects you more with other people than practicing gratitude in your life. Each day is a gift, and you cannot take anything in this life for granted. Taking time in your day to be thankful for what you have reminds you that you have a lot more than you realize.

2. *Practice humility.* Being human means having an ego, but sometimes to get back in touch with what really matters, it is better to practice humility. It does not mean putting yourself below others; it means letting go of your need to be above them. Help other people without expecting anything in return, and see what happens.

3. *Practice optimism.* Believe that good things will happen if you focus on having a proactive state of mind. This causes good things to happen! When you put your energy into being optimistic about the thing that you are doing, there will not be any negative outcomes, because you will always see the positive in the experience.

70 Karl Albrecht, Ph.D., The (Only) Seven Spiritual Principles We Need to Succeed, https://www.psychologytoday.com/blog/brainsnacks/201301/the-only-seven-spiritual-principles-we-need-succeed

4. *Practice generosity.* Being a generous person means giving more than is expected whenever you are given the opportunity. Having a generous attitude means sharing yourself, your resources, and your life with the people in your life that surround you. It helps you connect to others and fulfills your spirit.

5. *Practice forgiveness.* There is no point harboring ill will towards people because they have wronged you. Forgive and forget, and you will be happier and healthier for it. This will help you get back in touch with who you are and what makes you happy.

As you can tell, practice is the catalyst that ignites the spirit. In order to get in touch with your spirituality, practice these simple actions and feel your internal spirit thrive.

Connectedness and Spirituality

Modern life often leaves us feeling harassed, overly busy, and stressed. Life can often seem like a blur of mundane experiences that never seem to change. Spiritual connectedness can change this for you. When you feel spiritually connected, life seems to go a lot more smoothly, problems vanish, and you feed off the inspiration that is all around you.

Instead of feeling isolated and sad, you feel connected, like a working part in some giant cosmic plan. Understanding your place in the plan is all part of figuring out your spirituality. Connection, you see, is what brings people together. When you are connected to others and to the world, you gain access to a lot more strength, balance, and wisdom than one person can keep to themselves.

Connectedness helps your inner strength grow when you need it, and it becomes an endless source of energy all around you that you can tap into as needed. When you feel connected, you understand that things happen for a reason. Destiny becomes more than a concept and instead becomes a reality. Tapping into this "collective unconscious" is where universal knowledge lies.

It helps you put the world into a much more logical perspective. When you feel this connectivity, you know that to harm anyone or anything is wrong—because it would be like harming yourself. To tap into this, I highly recommend the practice of meditating.

People spend their whole lives searching for meaning and connectedness when they have access to it from within from the day that they are born. You can get in touch with this feeling through music, yoga, exercise, prayer, meditation, fasting, and by being in natural surroundings.

If you want to improve[71] the quality of your experience here on earth, then you will understand that tapping into this connectedness can be a transcendent experience. Artists, writers, and other creatives tap into it regularly to help them create new ideas and forms of knowledge.

Spirituality is all about feeling the connection that we have with each other and with the world. It is a direct line from your internal life to the cosmos—and you only need the desire and daily practice to realize it.

The Life Balance Mindset

Having a life balance mindset will take you wherever you need to go in this life. That is why, over the years, I have developed a life balance assessment to help you determine where you are on your journey.

Take a moment of your time to better acquaint yourself with your current values, morals and ethics, and those activities and attitudes that you use on a regular basis. When you take my life balance assessment, you are given a form and asked to answer each question truthfully, even if it hurts.

---

71   Vanessa Cordoniu, Got Spirit? Five Simple Ways to Feel Spiritually Connected NOW, http://www.selfgrowth.com/articles/got-spirit-five-simple-ways-to-feel-spiritually-connected-now

The outcome of the test is to assess your current actions and thinking, not merely what you would like to be or should be doing. On completion, my clients will add up the amount of true responses for each category—awarding themselves 10% for each true response.

It is important at that stage to recognize one's strengths in particular energy domains that hold the highest scores. These categories are the domains that will be more challenging to break into when creating your future life balance activities.

The activities I am speaking about help people find their way to their true selves using the Equality of Five Principle. A life balance mindset means that you are dedicated to ensuring that each of your energy domains is being nurtured.

Things get much easier when you realize that each of your energy areas is being influenced by all of these internal and external factors each day. Living with life balance in mind all the time ensures that you are always fully charged and ready for life's challenges.

Your mind will be resilient to external influences, your emotions grounded and protected, your body healthy and fit, and your relationships strong. Finally, your life will be guided by your spirit—a voice that has been wanting to show you where your place is in this world. I firmly believe that we all have one!

Adopt a life balance mindset today by working through my life balance assessment to see where your shortcomings are. Together we can improve your life and return you to your natural state of universal connection, strength, and purpose.

Life Balance Advantage

Please take a moment of your time to better acquaint us with your current values, activities, and attitudes to which you are committed. The way to use this form successfully is to answer it honestly and truthfully. We are looking for what you are currently doing or thinking, not merely what you would like to be doing or should be doing!

MANAGING <u>PHYSICAL ENERGY</u>
(True or False)

1. I go to bed and wake up early each day, getting **7–8 hours of sleep** per night for optimal functioning.

2. I go to sleep and wake up consistently at the **same times.**

3. I consistently eat a **balanced, healthy diet,** consuming daily: 5-6 small, low-calorie, highly nutritious meals, ensuring a steady resupply of glucose and essential nutrients.

4. I attend regular **physical and dental checkups** yearly.

5. I can fall asleep quickly and easily **without preferring bedtime distractions** like the TV, cell phones, Facebook and other social media, radio, lights left on, etc.

6. I maximize my consumption of **fruits and vegetables**.

7. I drink 48 to 64 ounces of **water daily**.

8. I **avoid eating after 8 p.m.** in the evening.

9. I do not smoke and refrain from the **unhealthy use** of drugs or alcohol.

10. I **safely escalate my heart rate**, performing a minimum of 2-3 aerobic, cardiovascular workouts weekly.

% of TRUE responses: _____
(10 possible responses)

MANAGING <u>EMOTIONAL ENERGY</u>

(True or False)

1. I acknowledge both **happy and painful memories**.

2. I can access my **positive emotional energy** by utilizing self-confidence, self-control, interpersonal effectiveness, and empathy.

3. I notice when **my negative emotions are costing me energy** and impacting my performance and can consequentially readjust my thoughts and feelings.

4. I can consistently **identify** and distinguish one emotion from another.

5. I can consistently and courageously **express** all my different emotions, both positive and negative.

6. I listen to my **inner self talk**.

7. I exercise my emotional muscles by **pushing past my current** emotional limits and utilizing patience, empathy, and confidence.

8. I have a **non-judgmental** attitude.

9. I can openly **express both tears and laughter**.

10. I can detect when I am experiencing **stress overload**.

% of TRUE responses: _____
(10 possible responses)

MANAGING <u>MENTAL ENERGY</u>
(True or False)

1. I use my mental energy to better organize my life and **focus my attention.**
2. Considering my school/work demands, I use my mental energy to engage life while remaining **realistically optimistic** and always working towards a positive outcome or solution.
3. I am capable of supporting myself by practicing **positive self-talk,** effective time management, positive visualization, and mental preparation.
4. **I follow through and work on decisions** with clarity and action steps.
5. I can **accept** circumstances beyond my control.
6. I realize that **physical exercise** stimulates cognitive ability.
7. I consistently practice stress **management and mental relaxation techniques** (i.e., meditation, guided imagery, positive visualization)
8. I realize that when I lack the mental awareness necessary to perform at my best, I must **systematically build my mental capacity** by pushing past my comfort zone.
9. I am **open and receptive** to new ideas and life patterns.
10. I use my **imagination** in considering new choices or possibilities.

% of TRUE responses: _____
(10 possible responses)

MANAGING INTERPERSONAL ENERGY

(True or False)

1. **I share my opinions and feelings** without seeking the approval of others or fearing negative results.

2. I create and **proactively participate** in satisfying relationships while maintaining ongoing communications (phone contacts, greeting cards, visits, etc.)

3. In my relationships, I can recognize my needs and desires and am capable of **sustaining intimacy, both physical and emotional.**

4. I maintain a **balance** between my school/work and time with friends/family.

5. I maintain **clear boundaries** with loved ones, avoiding communicating on behalf of relatives or friends who find it difficult to talk for themselves.

6. I am clear in **expressing my needs and desires**, even when it requires that I communicate my uncomfortable emotions (frustration, anger, love).

7. I am open and **honest** with people without fearing the consequences.

8. I **focus on the positive aspects** of my relationships.

9. I am capable of **identifying my internal feelings** and honestly communicating them in my relationships.

10. I am capable of being honest and direct **when communicating to authority figures** (teachers, bosses, coaches, etc.).

% of TRUE responses: _____

(10 possible responses)

MANAGING <u>SPIRITUAL ENERGY</u>

(True or False)

1. I realize that **spiritual energy provides the force** for action in all dimensions of my life. It fuels my passion, commitment, integrity, and honesty.

2. I understand that spiritual energy is derived from a **connection to my deeply-held values** and living life with a focus beyond my own self-interest.

3. I have experienced that character; **the courage and conviction to live by my deepest values** is central to maintaining my spiritual energy.

4. I often **feel so connected** to the people around me that it appears as if there is no separation between us.

5. I realize that **apathy, resignation, declining self-esteem, and a lack of life direction** can be signs of depleted spiritual energy.

6. I believe that **miracles happen**.

7. I live in the "**here and now**"—the present moment.

8. I know that I am **more than** just my internal thoughts or physical being.

9. I often have unexpected **flashes of insight** or understanding while relaxing.

10. I have had moments of great joy in which I suddenly had a clear, **deep feeling of oneness** with all that exists.

% of TRUE responses: _____
(10 possible responses)

The Darkest Enemies in Your Life

Gaining a life balance advantage means seizing control of the many dark enemies in your life. I had many growing up, and some stayed with me all the way until early adulthood, causing numerous problems, confusion, and stress—and at times had me questioning the value of my life!

- *My physical domain:* As a child, I can remember many moments of stress-induced illnesses as a result of a life fraught with imbalances. At age 12, I suffered third degree burns all over my body and spent significant time in the hospital. Later, during my adolescent years, like many teenagers, my life centered around the use of alcohol, tobacco, and substances to self-medicate from the emotional and mental stressors that plagued me. Having never been taught to value exercise and proper nutrition, I lived a sedentary life fraught with overpowering negative emotions.

- *My emotional domain:* During most of my young adult life, I was challenged by anxiety and panic attacks, accompanied by moments in my childhood and adolescence when I found myself depressed and feeling quite helpless. There were rare moments when I perseverated on thoughts of self-harm in the hope of escaping the dark emotions that plagued me.

- *My mental domain:* In my childhood and young adult years, I was obsessed with negative thoughts, almost overpowered by them at times. The only strategy I knew was self-medicating them away. Sharing my emotions and asking for help was uncommon and uncomfortable to me. The only way I believed that I could control such negative thinking was to self-medicate in order to escape my own negative thinking.

- *My interpersonal domain:* Like so many other adolescents and young adults, I experienced considerable social loneliness.

Some of my significant relationships ended with abrupt rejection, abandonment, and considerable emotional distress. There were times of significant family dysfunction around communication and substance misuse, which certainly darkened my earlier years. Then in adulthood, at age 33, I lost my first son, Gavin Marcus, to Sudden Infant Death Syndrome. The loss of Gavin at only 7 ½ weeks left me with inconsolable grief and feelings of loss and desertion.

- *My spiritual domain:* Having had significant religious faith during much of my childhood was certainly a blessing, yet I spent many years within my family feeling lost, lonely, and alone. I had lacked a healthy relationship with myself, others, and the universe. I lacked trust, forgiveness, and a zest for life. My awareness lacked an inner longing or sense of my true purpose in life. Yet I always possessed an inward, hidden, deep personal longing, an urge to know in a special way.

These were my darkest enemies that I had to learn to overcome. You will have a set of your own too. The darkest enemies of all are the ones we excuse away, but we know they do us harm. Which of these are yours?

- Drugs, alcohol, food, sex, unhealthy relationships, money, shopping, gambling, social media and obsessive technology, negative thinking, self-doubt, procrastination, and resentment

The Five Facts of Human "Being"

To be human and live a successful human life, you have to have all of your five domains in sync. If they are not in sync, time and time again your energy will be out of balance, triggering a total collapse of your inner self.

Being human means being balanced. We have to take each side of ourselves into account because we are the sum total of each of these parts. Without a healthy body, our minds will not work effectively.

Unhealthy food choices will poison our cell tissue and welcome in a state of disease.

Without a healthy mind, our bodies will degenerate, and our emotions will turn against us—causing untold harm to our internal selves. The same can be said about the lack of a healthy spirit; being unfulfilled is no way to live. It sometimes creates the absence of emotion, which can become intolerable.

To be balanced and to really seek out our purpose as human beings, we must dedicate ourselves to the consistent rebalancing required to keep us growing and becoming our true selves. When you are functioning at peak performance, there is nothing that you cannot do.

When I cleaned up my act and balanced my life—taking all five domains into account—I finally recognized what it was to be a human being. Because life is constantly in motion, if you allow it to stagnate or if you allow your energy to become disrupted, you are going to be plagued with pain and adversity in life.

Most adversity comes from within; this is the outright truth of life. In order to be a successful "being," you have to continually work at it. Every day is accompanied by a new challenge that you have to embrace.

Balancing your life is about an ongoing pursuit for high performance living. You will eat right, exercise, and rest every single day. You will take time to care for your emotions every single day. You will make sure your thoughts are positive and working for you every single day. And you will ensure that your relationships are being nurtured every single day.

Finally, when you can tend to your spiritual needs daily, your life will explode into the success and happiness that you have always wanted. Life will finally be the beautiful, happy place that other people have always told you it can be. You will finally become aware that you can self-heal through Life Balance—so that you can own the happiness you deserve and know you are blessed.

PART IV

TAKE 5:
STRATEGIES FOR
TOTAL HUMAN
HEALTH

CHAPTER 10
FACT #1: CREATING PHYSICAL BALANCE

"To keep the body in good health is a duty...otherwise we shall not be able to keep our mind strong and clear."
Buddha

You only get one body in this life, and what you put into it will either keep it healthy and happy or make it sick and difficult to live with. In part four, we will be working through a host of strategies to help you maintain human health across all five life balance domains.

In this chapter, we begin by covering how to create physical balance in your body. There is much that can be done to get your body back in shape, and once you have done it, you will be primed for performance in other areas of your life.

The Ravages of Stress on Your Body

What if I told you that stress is killing you? You have been totally unaware of it, but stress has been costing you physical health, emotional and mental stability, healthy relationships, and spiritual alignment. It is your number one dark enemy!

When stress becomes chronic in your daily life, it overloads your body's systems—silently and systematically sabotaging your physical health. Stress-related disease is everywhere that you look. Until stress is completely released, it stays lodged in your body, causing your cells to run rampant and putting your health at risk.

Imagine skipping a rent payment and not having the money to afford rent that month. Suddenly, anxiety and worry set in. You cannot sleep, so your energy bottoms out. You cannot work because you are so worried, and procrastination sets in.

Your amygdala in your midbrain senses danger, so it initiates your body's fight or flight response to stress. Your body releases adrenaline and the stress hormone cortisol, which diverts blood from your digestive tract. Now you are less able to digest food and absorb life-giving nutrients. You gain weight.

In this heightened state, your brain's creative center is deemed nonessential and shuts down. It decreases your problem solving ability, creative skill, and intuition. You feel increasingly irritable, isolated, and impatient. Then your relationships suffer!

Your metabolism slows down, and you get sick. By the time you have fixed the rent problem, you are depleted, exhausted, and depressed. You forget about exercising and eating right. Chronic pain and headaches set in. Suddenly it is a stress-induced[72] breakdown.

---

72   The Signs and Symptoms of a Nervous Breakdown You Should Not Ignore, http://
www.professional-counselling.com/nervousbreakdown_panic_attack.html#.VQWKX_
mUepc

Choose Live Foods: Your Body Matters

As I mentioned before, there are two types of food: living food and dead food. Dead food is what you currently focus on eating all the time right now. I know this because 90% of the modern American diet is made up of dead food. Live food consists of fresh fruits and vegetables and leafy green items. This is where you get real nutrients from!

Living food is different from raw food because it has a higher enzyme content. Living foods are generally best eaten raw, though, so they often get confused with "raw food" in general. To sustain life and get the full life-force of the plant you are eating, it needs to be raw.

Eating 75-100%[73] live foods means dedicating yourself to nutritionally dense, organic, uncooked, and unprocessed food. These foods will also help alkaline your body. When you eat a lot of cooked food, you consume acidic toxins faster than your body can eliminate them, so they back up. This disrupts your body's natural acid/alkaline balance.

Your body is like an alkaline battery that runs on electrons. When energy flows between these, that is when your body is in peak shape. Eating lots of uncooked live foods will pack your body with nutrients and enzymes, and these are excellent for your health.

Not only will you lose weight but your body will shift from a perpetual state of starvation into a more natural state of satiation. You will become less hungry and feel the need to binge eat far less. When you eat the right things, your body regulation kicks back in.

Live food[74] also contains a lot of enzymes, and you need these to correctly digest your food. Metabolic, digestive, and food enzymes will help keep nutrients being absorbed in your body. By incorporating living foods into your diet, you can reap the benefits of improving

---

73   The Science of Raw Food, http://www.rawfoodlife.com/#axzz3USgVDWri
74   Live Foods, https://experiencelife.com/article/live-foods/

your nutrition and your nutritional uptake and making sure that your body is alkaline.

Disease and dysfunction thrive in an acidic body, so this is extremely beneficial. Remember to load up in small portions today on sprouts, peppers, onions, radishes, salad, oranges, plums, pineapples, and other nutrient-rich fruits!

Live to Move: Motion Creates Energy

It is no secret—motion creates energy in your body, and we could all use more of it due to our stressful lives. When you have sorted out your diet and have been eating correctly, the next logical thing to do is to look at your exercise regimen.

If you hate exercise, it is because your body feels foreign doing it. The human body actually loves to move, but you have to find your unique exercise style so that you can stick with it over time; otherwise you will give up and be back to square one.

Daily exercise is something that needs to become part of your life—period! It has been proven that exercise reduces your risk for a number of serious diseases, plus it greatly reduces the impact of stress on your body.

But exercise also creates positive[75] energy, which makes you feel good. It has been scientifically proven that exercising lifts your spirits and makes you happier because of the endorphin release that you get after exercising.

You do not want to over-exercise however. An hour a day, every day, of moderate to intense exercise is all that is needed for you to maintain a healthy body and generate the energy you need to stay motivated, happy, and engaged all day long.

The best part is that the more you exercise, the more your body needs that exercise. After skipping a few days of exercise after just a

---

75 Leo Widrich, What Happens to Our Brains When We Exercise and How It Makes Us Happier, https://blog.bufferapp.com/why-exercising-makes-us-happier

few short months, you will feel it. And you will not like it, because your body will miss the endorphin rush!

Daily exercise[76] helps prevent disease, it improves your stamina, and it strengthens and tones your body. This prepares your body for the rigors of daily life and to survive through periods of intense stress.

Exercise also improves your flexibility, controls your weight, and improves your quality of life. Forty minutes a day of cardio and twenty minutes a day of resistance training is all you need to keep your body in ideal condition.

Practical Strategies: Stress Control

How do you control stress in your daily life? There are many practical strategies that you can employ. At any given time, use one of these to reduce your toxic stress burden.

- *Keep a journal, and write things down that bother you.* Tracking what stresses you out can lead to elimination of that thing and will help you reduce your stress levels.
- *Talk about your stress with a friend.* Talk, laugh, and cry with a friend to communicate the stress that you are working through. This will make you feel better.
- *Practice specific breathing techniques[77] for stress reduction.* It will slow your heart rate, lower your blood pressure, and reduce the activity of stress hormones in the blood.
- *Jump on a treadmill or bike.* Short-burst exercise activities are excellent for instantly reducing stress, as they expend nervous, negative energy.
- *Meditate daily.* Sit comfortably, and calm your mind. Listen within to a meaningless word or mantra (i.e., "shiring") while

---

76   Armand Tecco, Why Is Exercise Important?, http://www.healthdiscovery.net/articles/exercise_importa.htm
77   Relaxation Techniques: Try These Steps to Reduce Stress, http://www.mayoclinic.org/healthy-living/stress-management/in-depth/relaxation-technique/art-20045368

merely allowing your thoughts to flow alongside the mantra. Simply favor the sound of the mantra as your thoughts come and go.

- *Read a book.* Like you are doing now, pick up a good book and read it! Reading can reduce your stress load by 68%[78] because it invites your mind into another reality.

- *Listen to music.* Music helps you control your emotions, so slow music will calm you and guide you into a better frame of mind. Avoid listening to violent music. Remember, garbage in, garbage out!

- *Spend time in nature.* Nature is a great place to reconnect with your spirit and who you are. Hang out among greenery, and breathe in the fresh air.

- *Have a massage.* Stress causes muscle tension, so getting a massage allows that tension to be released. Often the trauma of everyday living requires that it be released from your cell tissue.

- *Do not eat sugar.* Sugar might relieve stress while you are enjoying it, but soon after, there is a crash that leaves you worse off. Cut out all sugar to reduce your stress.

- *Hug a pet.* Studies show that loving a pet can reduce stress significantly, so do not feel like you are wasting time when you play with Fido or hug your kitten.

Practical Strategies: The Balanced Diet

A balanced diet these days is a tough thing to get right, mainly because what the government claims is "balanced" is usually just a bunch of dead food and low-quality grains that make you fat and unhealthy.

---

78 Chris Bailey, 9 Stress Relief Strategies That Actually Work, http://alifeofproductivity. com/9-stress-relief-strategies-that-actually-work/

In fact, you should focus on nutrients, nutrient uptake, and eating minimal meat—only quality sources of meat to sustain you on your balanced diet. This means:

- Healthy sources of fish.
- Free range chicken.
- No animal products that have been given routine antibiotics, hormones, or chemicals.
- Lean protein sources only.
- Free range, organic eggs.
- Organic vegetables with normal levels of pesticide (wash thoroughly).
- Organic fruits with normal levels of pesticide.

Here is the toxic reality. We are killing ourselves by consuming truckloads of hidden sugar. Despite decades of Americans being programed into thinking that fat is evil, it turns out sugar—not fat—is what makes you sick and overweight.

Beyond question, sugar in all its forms is the root cause of our obesity epidemic and most of the chronic diseases. Many illnesses are caused by sugar: heart disease, cancer, dementia, type-2 diabetes, depression, and even acne.

The average American consumes about 152 pounds of sugar a year. That is roughly 22 teaspoons every day for every person in America. Our kids consume about 34 teaspoons every day— and believe it or not, flour is even worse than sugar. We consume about 146 pounds of flour a year, which raises blood sugar even more than table sugar.

Another outrageous fact: Sugar is eight times as addictive as cocaine.

Being addicted to sugar and flour is not an emotional eating disorder. It is a biological disorder, driven by hormones and neurotransmitters that fuel sugar and carb cravings—leading to uncontrolled overeating. It is the reason nearly 70 percent of Americans and 40 percent of kids are overweight.[79]

- Do you eat when you are not hungry?
- Do you experience a food trance after eating?
- Do you feel bad about your eating habits or avoid certain activities because of your eating?
- Do you get withdrawal symptoms if you cut down or stop eating sugar or flour?

Now that you are no longer sleepwalking on this issue, take the healthy **6 Steps Challenge:**

1. Stop consuming all forms of sugar, flour products, and artificial sweeteners, which cause increased cravings and slow metabolism and lead to fat storage. Stick to real, whole, fresh food.

2. Do not drink your calories. Any form of liquid sugar calories is worse than solid food with sugar or flour. Think of it as mainlining sugar directly to your liver.

3. Think about eating protein at every meal—especially breakfast—which is the key to balancing blood sugar and insulin and cutting cravings.

4. Eat the right carbs. Did you know that vegetables are carbs? And you get to eat as much as you want—only the non-starchy veggies such as greens, anything in the broccoli family (cauliflower, kale, collards), asparagus, green beans, mushrooms, onions, zucchini, tomatoes, fennel, eggplant, artichokes, and peppers.

5. Along with protein, have good fats at every meal and snack, including nuts and seeds, extra virgin olive oil, coconut butter, avocados, and omega-3 fats from fish.

---

79   Mark Hyman. How to Detox From Sugar in 10 Days. http://drhyman.com/blog/2014/03/06/top-10-big-ideas-detox-sugar/

6. Sleep deprivation drives sugar and carb cravings by affecting your appetite hormones. Sleep is the best way to fight against the drive to overeat.

Practical Strategies: Medicine and Health

For every pill that you take, there is a consequence. If you have been raised to believe it is fine to pop a painkiller or five for a mild headache or any ache or pain, then you need a reality check. Pill popping has an incredible impact on your body.

Take stock of the medications that you take every day. Do these help or hinder your daily performance? You should be mindful if your pill taking is habitual. Chronic medication for an ailment is one thing, but there are many kinds of medication people buy over the counter, and these are abused and overused for little reason.

The psychiatric industry,[80] for example, overprescribes medication and keeps people on it for too long. Just recently federal investigators found evidence of widespread overuse of psychiatric drugs by older Americans with Alzheimer's disease. The truth is that psychiatric medication overuse in America is rife.

People go to their therapist and walk out too freely with prescriptions for antidepressants, antipsychotics, and sleeping pills. Children are even falling prey to this; many of them are on three or four medications before the age of ten.

Medication is not what the medical industry is supposed to be about. Most ailments can be helped or cured with natural medicines that do little or no damage to the body. Modern medicines almost always have side effects. You take one medication for a year and then two more problems arise from that medication. Before you know it, you are taking five pills a day.

---

80   Robert Pear, Psychiatric Drug Overuse Is Cited by Federal Study, http://www.nytimes.com/2015/03/02/us/psychiatric-drug-overuse-is-cited-by-federal-study.html?_r=0

Take some time to consider the medication that you have been prescribed. Get second, third, and fourth opinions. Never allow anyone to tell you that you have to take a specific pill. Always question what they say and why.

Medicine and health are growing apart because of profiteering agents in the pharmaceutical field. They want to sell drugs—and a lot of them. Just keep in mind that many of your ailments can be healed naturally. Investigate this and find out how.

Practical Strategies: Villain Removal

If you have a villain in your life, it might be time to remove him. That means limiting your exposure to television and the advertising racket, which exists to sell you things that you do not need. Above all, ignore the messages from psychiatric companies.

If you are on psychiatric medication, as many people these days are, consider your options. Health personnel are diagnosing people in less than an hour and keeping them on serious medications for years with little actual therapy to help the patient recover.

What you are never told is that this medication will not totally cure you of your ailment, whether it is a mood disorder or depression. Medication works in the beginning, and then—like a villain—you run the risk of becoming addicted to it and can start causing damage in your body.

Many psychiatric[81] patients develop diabetes, obesity, and other chronic diseases from the weight gain involved in these tablets. You would be better off controlling certain psychiatric disorders with nutrition and exercise than with psychiatric drugs.

These villains will be thrust in your path, and you will have to take a stand to remove them. Psychiatric medication can do terrible damage to your mental processes and your emotions, and it can

---

81 What We Can Do About the Overuse of Psychiatric Medications, http://corinnawest.com/what-we-can-do-about-the-overuse-of-psychiatric-medications/

destroy your spirit. At times, you will not even recognize who you have become.

Visit your doctor, and ask if you can be weaned off your medication. Give them good reasons why, and say that you want to try natural methods of control. If your doctor does not listen, then move to a more open-minded physician who offers additional natural options.

A villain is an element of control in your life that has been imposed on you that you do not need. It does nothing but drain your energy and keep you locked into a dance of ill health. You have to decide if you are taking part in this dance or stepping out of it.

The villains in your life can include drugs, food, alcohol, gambling, promiscuous sex, obsessive social media and technology, and other unhealthy behaviors. You must stop these negative behaviors if you are going to find life balance.

Practical Strategies: Rest and Recharge

Looking after yourself is priority number one for you now. One of the most important elements of physical balance concerns rest. You need to know when your body has been overworked and needs to rest and relax to restore the energy you need to continue.

- Get enough sleep![82] Everyone is different, but it usually means getting between six to eight hours of good, quality sleep every night. This will restore you and help reset your mind for the new day. Never underestimate the power of quality sleep!

- Take slow walks. Nothing restores the mind and body quicker than a leisurely 20-minute stroll through a scenic area. Take them daily, and enjoy them.

- Contrary to popular belief, watching television or movies is not rest. What also falls into this category is obsessive social media

---

82   Sleep Hack: A Simple Strategy for Better Rest in Less Time, http://www.lifehack.org/articles/lifehack/sleep-hack-a-simple-strategy-for-better-rest-in-less-time.html

and technology. It keeps the mind active and the body sedentary and should not be done for more than two consecutive hours. It can even keep you awake long after the media has been shut off!

- Many top executives have a meditation chair. This is where they can go when they need to do nothing for 30 minutes. Spend the time relaxing, breathing, stretching, and enjoying doing absolutely nothing. The only rules are to not think about work, stress, or anything else.

- When you finish an intensive task, remind yourself to take small breaks during your day, even if you are at work. Never move seamlessly from one thing to the next or you will exhaust your brain. For every hour worked, 10 minutes should be rest. If you work for two consecutive hours, rest for 20 minutes.

- Take up a relaxing activity like sailing or fishing. This allows you to get out into nature, sit quietly, and enjoy the activity.

- Take a coffee break, without the coffee. Switch to decaf or enjoy some tea as you take much-needed coffee breaks at work or at home.

Rest and relaxation is deceptively important to your overall health and physical wellbeing. If you do not recover from the things you do in good time, they will compound, and you may experience fatigue and eventual burnout because you did not look after yourself enough.

CHAPTER 11
FACT #2: BECOMING EMOTIONALLY CENTERED

"Every day we have plenty of opportunities to get angry, stressed or offended. But what you're doing when you indulge these negative emotions is giving something outside yourself power over your happiness. You can choose to not let little things upset you."

Joel Osteen

The process of becoming emotionally centered is exciting and terrifying all at once. Until now you may have had problems with your emotions, but this is your turning point. Today you are going to learn how to manage your emotions so that they do not get the better of you.

Moving from being an emotional wreck to being emotionally centered is a life-changing experience, and all you need to do is practice some of these strategies. They will help you maintain self-awareness and rein in the wilder parts of your emotional state.

Being an Emotional Wreck: The Toll

If, like many other people, your emotional side[83] often gets the better of you, you are used to being in a perpetual state of wreckage. When all of your emotions are tied into a great big ball of confusion, this is when you become an emotional wreck.

You stop responding to people and experiences in the right ways, and your heightened sensitivity for things leaves you distraught at the best of times. This is no way to live, and it comes from not correctly dealing with your emotions as they arise.

There is a real toll involved with allowing yourself to be an emotional wreck all the time. You will feel exhausted all day, burned out, and lifeless. As a result, you may retreat to distraction,[84] watching TV, being online, or avoiding people.

You might medicate to make yourself feel better. Alcohol, chocolate, shopping, or gambling—these all numb your pain, but not forever. Overanalyzing your emotions is also a negative behavior as it holds you in a traumatic moment.

Blame is another popular side effect of being emotionally traumatized. None of these make you feel better, and you are only pushing yourself further into the pity party of despair. Your health, mental state, and spirit will all suffer, not to mention your relationships most of all!

The Value of Emotional Intelligence

Defined as the ability to manage yourself, emotional intelligence[85] means that people that possess a strong self-awareness of their

---

83 Janet Louise Stephenson, Choosing NOT to Be an Emotional Wreck, http://www. butterfly-maiden.com/personal-development/emotional-wreck

84 What to Do When You're an Emotional Wreck, http://coachingwithroy.com/what-to-do-when-youre-an-emotional-wreck/

85 Russell Razzaque, The Universal Value of Emotional Intelligence, https://www. psychologytoday.com/blog/political-intelligence/201206/the-universal-value-emotional-intelligence

emotions know how to manage them correctly. Because you have woken up recently, this needs to be your new goal.

The most common cause for anxiety in our modern culture is that reason (head) and emotions (heart) are out of balance. Employers would benefit if they hired managers on the emotional side and employees on the rational side. Then employees would not be too emotional to cause foolish actions, and managers would not be so rational that they begin with the wrong premise and, using unique logic, come up with an incorrect answer.

Both the head and the heart need a master. Through personal initiative, the ego behaves via "trained will" and is the presiding judge over emotions and reason. In the absence of "trained will," the ego minds its own business and allows the head and heart to fight it out. This causes internal conflict!

Some 95% of adults never manage to lift themselves from their adolescent need to "belong" to the group. But successful people always follow independent lives surrounded by a small group of like-minded people.

Think about how you feel most of the time. Do life events get to you? Your relationships? The amount of money that you have in your bank account? You are the only one alive that can determine how these things impact you. You decide how to feel. It all relies on how you have chosen to internally communicate with yourself.

Nothing in the world has any meaning unless you give it some. That is a fundamental truth. Emotional intelligence is about being aware of this 24/7 and choosing to remain calm. This choice takes years to develop, but you must use your head to keep your heart in line.

Emotional intelligence is about knowing when to indulge in your feelings and when to put them aside for your own benefit and the benefit of others. Life will never stop pushing your buttons, so you can choose to either roll with it or be traumatized by it!

Devastation Caused by Negativity, Rejection, and Fear!

Emotions suffer when faced with negativity, rejection, and fear. Of all the enemies in the world, these three will wreck your emotions sooner than nearly anything else. You have to learn that this devastation can be controlled.

FEAR was originally a response in human beings where quick action would protect us from danger and harm. These days FEAR can be defined as False Evidence Appearing Real. You need to learn to overcome this FEAR.

When you switch into an emotional state that activates your nervous system, you are forced to pay attention to it—and fight or flight mode kicks in. People have two great fears: the fear of failure and the fear of success. These drive everything we do and everything we are.

You need to condition[86] yourself to make it hard for you to feel bad and easy for you to feel good. When you are fearful, zone in on it. Recognize that it is there, breathe, and let go of it. When it comes again, recognize that your mind needs reassurance and tenderness. Then when it comes again, replace this fear with love. It works every time.

Rejection is also a big one and can cause devastation on your emotions. The funny thing is, life is all about rejection; you cannot have acceptance without it! You can only feel rejected if you internally allow yourself to feel this way—remember that.

Buddha once said that if someone offers you a gift and you decline it, to whom does the gift belong? To the person who offered it. In the same way, if you do not accept people's gift of abuse, to whom does it belong? Not you.

---

86   Overcoming F.E.A.R.: False Evidence Appearing Real, http://www.awaken. com/2013/01/overcoming-f-e-a-r-false-evidence-appearing-real/

Handling rejection is the key to life successes. JK Rowling, author of the Harry Potter series, was rejected by 12 different publishers before placing her book. Sylvester Stallone was turned down by 1,000 producers, so he wrote and starred in his own movie. People told him he could not do that, but he did, and the famous Rocky series was born.

Without rejection, there can be no learning, and to learn is the key to everything. Failure is the same—if you do not fail, you cannot learn how to get it right. Do not allow your emotions to become influenced by the learning tools of FEAR, negativity, and rejection. Accept the lessons that life offers you, and stay calm.

Practical Strategies: The Emotional System

There are lot of ways that you can enhance your emotional system to become more aware of how it works. The more you know, the better off you are because you will notice when something good, or something bad, has been triggered inside you.

You need to learn[87] how to identify and communicate your feelings. It is a proven fact that if you spend every day journaling about positive experiences, you will reduce worry and increase your performance by 10-15%. Imagine that!

The expression of genes is crucial, and that expression is controlled by the energetic choices that we make through things like emotions. All negative emotions are a result of a disruption in the body's energetic system.

When an assault on our physical or emotional integrity happens— whether physical or verbal or a result of our own inner fears and scary self-talk—it does not matter. It throws up a stop switch that causes a massive energy disruption and can cause energetic chaos.

---

87   5 Ways Keeping a Journal Can Help You De-Stress, http://www.huffingtonpost.com/2013/02/13/5-ways-keeping-a-journal-_n_2671735.html

Unlocking this block in an energy pathway is like trying to bring light back to a building that has just had a blackout. Or you can liken it to a boulder that has rolled into a river and has caused the stream to stop flowing.

As long as the flow of water is diverted and the boulder is there, your emotions are not going to function well. Sometimes people are so riddled with energy boulders that they are seriously sensitive about everything.

Things like childhood pain, insult, or injury can cause a permanent disruption in the energy system that can seriously impact your health. This reshaped energy flow always results in physical or emotional pain that affects your health and wellbeing.

When this pain is triggered or reawakened, it can be felt as a primal fury well beyond the scope of what we understand about ourselves. Stored pain such as this is derived from incidents, or experiences, that we had when we were young and defenseless. When these negative "downloads" accumulate, fears and shame can have a lasting impact!

Practical Strategies: The Emotional Path & Identification

How you choose to harness your emotions in this life can either bring you great happiness or severe pain. To truly gain happiness and a sense of inner calm, you need be emotionally independent and gain a sense of maturity. That means knowing what you are feeling and why as well as how to responsibly express those feelings.

From time to time, we are all emotional hostages. Some people are locked away by the fear of intense emotions like inadequacy, rejection, and sadness, and for these individuals, nothing is worse than having to pick through the minefield of their own emotional triggers.

Many people never investigate their true potential because of their underlying emotional state. It prevents them from acting, taking risks, and reaching for something better. Still other people walk through life like a ticking time bomb, sensitive to any trigger. Their repressed emotion can cause them to react explosively without provocation or even from perceived slights.

People will do anything not to feel these emotions, including drinking and drugging them away. But it is important that we appreciate all of our emotions, even the bad ones. The key to emotional choice is learning to use emotions to achieve your life goals.

Appropriate identification[88] and expression of emotions is how it is done. All emotions are signals; you just need to know how to read them. That is why a key emotional process is identification. When and what we choose to identify with makes us who we are.

When you over-identify with something externally, you give away your essence, energy, and power to someone or something other than yourself. It is too easy to give this power away. But psychological identification can be turned on and off. You give something power when you identify with it, but you can choose not to do so.

Identification is usually an involuntary and unconscious process. Our life history and cultural programming have created these connections so that we can identify with things and people automatically. But situations change, and trauma occurs.

Think about that great sweater you loved and then ripped accidentally at a party. Will you involuntarily feel sad or angry?

Identification pulls your energy and makes you vulnerable to trauma. We suffer for purely symbolic reasons—like when we ding our car, or have a fight with our wife, or hear something bad about our religion. These are my things, so they hurt me. You must learn to distance yourself from this mindset to spare yourself the emotional trauma.

---

88   John D. Mayer, Glenn Geher, Emotional Intelligence and the Identification of Emotion, http://www.unh.edu/emotional_intelligence/EI%20Assets/Reprints...EI%20 Proper/EI1996MayerGeher.pdf

Practical Strategies: Avoiding Blissful Ignorance

It is true—we are all robots, conditioned to be a certain way. We live a life of routine habits and compulsions controlled by our psychological patterns or internal conditioning. All of us are prisoners of our unconscious drives, impulses, and needs.

To reach a state of serenity and peace, you have to embrace the reality that we are generally unconscious, completely asleep, and switched off to our own lives. This is the not-so-blissful ignorance we all exist in.

Your mind is inflexible and limited and can attach any thought to any emotion! Buddhists call this unconscious pattern of being asleep "samsara." While most people believe that they are in control of their daily happenings, this sleepwalking that we know is going on contradicts that belief.

Moving from one unconscious[89] trance to another is nothing more than preprograming. Our past shapes our current interpretation of reality, which means that we are all running on templates from our childhood or our past lives.

If you are watching a good TV show and someone is talking to you, do you listen? No, you do not, and this is what it is like. You have to turn your head away from the screen, refocus on what they are saying, and really listen in order to hear the message.

Communication happens on these two levels: the conscious and the unconscious. We get huge amounts of information from everywhere all day, so we sort it as best we can. Moving and engaging draws our attention the most.

A lot has been written about the common, everyday "trance" that occurs naturally in people. It is not bad for you unless it keeps you sleepwalking through life. In Eastern tradition, they talk about being trapped in "maya," a transient world of the mind—or the world of thoughts, feelings, and emotions.

---

89 Unconscious Ideas and Emotions, http://www.psychologistworld.com/emotion/emotion_5.php

Your identification and attachment to thoughts, feelings, or emotions can dictate your emotional state. Rather, you should be able to experience a multitude of natural trance states, which can lead you to a transcendental experience of yourself. Yet instead, we remain sleepwalkers, woken only by either pleasure or emotional pain as we move through life in a haze.

Practical Strategies: You Are Not Thoughts or Problems

Here is a shocking revelation: you are not your thoughts[90] or your problems! You have never been the things that pass through your conscious mind. You cannot be and will not ever be your thoughts, emotions, fears, memories, or ideas.

It is better to think of your emotional experience like this: imagine that you are in a puddle of mud and experiencing trouble getting out of it. The very second that you identify with that difficulty, your mental thinking pattern limits your freedom to transcend the challenge, similar to being confined inside a jail cell.

Once inside this cell, all resources are unavailable to you. These resources (i.e., the answers, resolutions, clarifications, explanations, and solutions that you need) cannot pass through the boundary of the jail cell, which is made up of belief. You are your difficulty.

The thing is...you are not. You can create as much distance as you need from that mud puddle to figure out the problem. You have simply been conditioned not to have this ability. Un-resourceful mental states like these cause narrowing, fixating of attention, and shrinking of your perspective. You experience things as "happening to you."

Each of these mental states, whether they are pleasant or unpleasant—like going on a nice, long vacation or getting into a mild

---

90   Greer Parry, Living Right Now: You Are Not Your Thoughts and Feelings, http://tinybuddha.com/blog/living-right-now-you-are-not-your-thoughts-and-feelings/

car accident—is comprised of unconscious, conditioned responses. It is these automated conditioned responses that have the potential to create adult problems that begin with the childhood experience.

Younger responses might have worked back then but do not work now. Natural absorption, or trance states, can be created as "symptoms," but they will need to be solved with a shift in internal perspective and attention. Instead of being fixated on a rigid emotional trigger response, start noticing the patterns in your emotional behavior.

Witness how things play out, and set yourself free from the continuous cycles that are no longer working to help you. With each mental image, sound, physical sensation, or sensory stimulus, you must begin to notice what sets your emotional state. The world is full of triggers that nurture pleasant and unpleasant feelings.

So you are not what your emotions might be dictating to you, and you can clear away old emotional baggage on your own. You simply need to notice your trigger, your pattern of behavior, and when you get a quiet moment, step away from the feelings to try to find a solution. Then, the next time it happens, use your new strategy instead.

Practical Strategies: Transcendence

What if I told you that you can transcend[91] these un-resourceful behaviors and thought patterns and change them with state and belief shifts in mindset? One of the most important things that make us human is our ability to exercise freedom of choice in everything we do.

We have the uniquely rich capacity to change and grow. In the swirling chaos that is stimulus and response, and very unlike Pavlov's dog, we have the blessed ability to choose our own personal response to external and internal happenings.

---

91 Tania Kotsos, Rise Above Your Emotions – Be the Witness Not the Puppet. http://www.mind-your-reality.com/above_your_emotions.html

We cannot change what happens to us in life, but we have always had the power to change our attitude towards the situation. As a human being, you have amazing power. You can develop the consciousness, which allows you to short circuit programmed responses.

That is right! You have the power to consciously alter your response to any stimulus. It can be the irritating and demanding voice of a family member or the infuriating non-verbal behaviors of a coworker that wants to see you fail. You do not have to become a mindless victim of your emotions, responding to the ching of that Pavlovian bell.

Human beings are not powerless[92] victims to their environmental surroundings, and while they bombard us with data from moment to moment, we decide how that impacts us. Learning to transcend your emotions is a tough job but a very, very useful skill.

You can choose to develop your internal bio-computer, your mind, to associate or disassociate from any trigger—internal or external. It is your choice. The challenge that faces most of us is our current state: we lack self-awareness.

You can develop these skills and become a master of your emotional states. All you have to do is develop a plan for maintaining your self-awareness through these trials and then be sure to execute your plan daily or as needed. Eventually, control will become a habit.

Whether you believe you can or you cannot, that is true. Be mindful, and acquire these skills. If you have the capability to think, then you have the capability to choose what you think. That means being able to control the boulders that tumble into your energy streams.

---

92   Transcending Our Reactive Emotions, http://www.innerfrontier.org/InnerWork/Archive/2014/20141006_Reactive_Emotions.htm

CHAPTER 12
FACT #3: ATTAINING MENTAL CLARITY

*"It is not your world that is shattering, but your
subjective map of what you believe this world to be"*
Mark Armiento

To attain mental clarity, you must understand how the mind works and how it can be either your greatest asset or your worst enemy. For most people, their mind on autopilot can be significant adversaries as they struggle to find a path to peace, success, and happiness.

Your mind is the computer system that governs every other action, emotion, thought, or experience that you have in your body. Learn to master it, and you will enjoy a lifetime of stronger relationships, greater successes, and enhanced experiences.

When Confusion and Indecision Reign

Unfortunately, when life has not been going well, you can find that your mind is not in the best shape. With anxiety and depression—even if these emotions are somewhat fleeting—you can get a host of accompanying mental dysfunctions that make your life harder.

If you stepped into a psychiatrist's office with symptoms of confusion and indecision, you would run the risk of being diagnosed with a serious mental illness and would be on your way armed with a prescription. But mental confusion comes from a complex overload of stimuli[93] that you become too fatigued to work through because you are so mentally exhausted.

There is nothing wrong with not being able to pick out the right suit for a party, but confusion often leads to perpetual indecision, and this can cause serious trouble for you upstairs. Your decision-making[94] ability will be reduced, which means that out of fear, you will become reluctant to move forward in life or change things for the better.

As you continue to stagnate, you will grow more confused! This is because you slip into a trance-like state of perpetual unhappiness, but you have no idea how to change it. When confusion and indecision reign, it means that you are suffering from mental fatigue.

Confusion and indecision are both signs that you are lost. Mentally, you cannot distance yourself from your reality or your problems, and so they are becoming mixed up inside you and are causing you trauma. When this happens, stop. Step back, and renew your mind.

Self-Respect and Self Definition: Tricky Concepts

How you define yourself helps determine how you treat yourself and think about yourself—so this is all tied into your self-concept.

---

93   Jude Bijou, Six Simple Steps to Cure Confusion, http://attitudereconstruction.com/2013/10/six-simple-steps-to-cure-confusion/
94   Decision Making and Indecisiveness Tendencies in Our Nature, http://www.charminghealth.com/applicability/decision-making.htm

Your perspective on how the world sees you can be so distorted and so at odds with how you feel inside that it can cause psychological difficulties.

We all need self-esteem to function, but your mind needs it most of all. Self-esteem, you see, is your mind's perception of how trustworthy it is. When you have low self-esteem because of negative external experiences, it reduces your quality of life.

Suddenly you do not respect yourself or what you think about the world. You feel like everything is "wrong" with you. You start to believe that you deserve the bad things that happen in your life. Your mind transforms into an instrument of torture. When you doubt your own mind, you sever an important internal trust that must exist in order for you to thrive.

Without self-respect and an adequate definition of yourself, you will not be able to overcome any challenges. Your perspective will be negative and defeatist, and you will revel in the predictable misery of it all.

Your values, your ethics, your morals—these are what truly matter, not anything from the external world. Evidence exists[95] that has proven that people who base their self-worth on what other people think suffer mental health consequences. This approval-based mindset will never make you happy; it demotivates you and makes you feel worthless.

Self-respect means having proper regard or dignity for yourself and your mind. Consider this your new golden rule. In the past, these concepts have been tricky because they have been used interchangeably with self-esteem and self-concept, but the truth is that respect is actually a very different thing altogether.

When you respect[96] your mind, you protect it from harm. You

---

95   Self-Esteem That's Based On External Sources Has Mental Health Consequences, Study Says, http://www.apa.org/monitor/dec02/selfesteem.aspx
96   Tonya Sheridan, The Forgotten Trait of Self-Respect, http://www.mindbodygreen. com/0-2800/The-Forgotten-Trait-of-SelfRespect.html

guard your thoughts and the thoughts other people propose. You are selective about the thoughts you decide are true, and you reject concepts that do not align with who you are. When you have self-respect, you know who you are and can define yourself. You need this for a strong, clear mind.

Mistakes Are Important: The Program That Failed You

In life there is always a balance—good versus evil, old versus new, and success versus failure. But one cannot exist without the other. In order to attain success, you need to learn, and learning requires friction.

The only way to generate friction[97] is to try to fail. You cannot have knowledge without failure, just like you cannot have light without any dark. So why have you been conditioned to loathe mistakes and fear failure? The employee system. Unfortunately, schools groom people to be great employees, which means a few things.

First of all, a good employee makes few mistakes. This is why we get tests at school, and it is why we are sorted into "smart" people and "not so smart" people. School trains you to fear failure because then you will be perceived publically as a fool or a "loser." But this is not reality at all! Failure is actually the most direct route to success.

I always say that life is 80% what not to do and the rest is about technique. The school program that you were hastened through failed you. It taught you how to be a great employee and little else. It taught you to fear authority, failure, and being "different" from everyone else. Ironically, it is usually those who are fearless and different that change the world.

Let's be honest; your mind needs to know what good judgment looks like in order to move forward. In any new field, you have to make

---

97   Ashley Fern, Why You Need to Learn From Your Mistakes, http://elitedaily.com/life/why-you-need-to-learn-from-your-mistakes/

mistakes to learn these lessons. Poor judgment and bad decisions are all part of the growth process.

What school failed to teach you was that "failure" is actually an invented concept. It does not exist in the real world unless you *decide* to give up on what you have been attempting to achieve. What you need to do now is to program yourself to fail more often. Take risks and try new things; never be afraid of the process of learning.

You can only make so many mistakes before you hit success. With time on your side, the odds are in your favor as long as you never give up. Your mind will understand this with every lesson learned. Never give up, never surrender—and you will never truly fail.

Practical Strategies: The Power of Belief

Reality is just a collection of your beliefs. What you perceive the world to be is not necessarily what it is. It is so true that whatever you believe, you can achieve. The mind is a tool for creation, and it can pull things into your life simply by wanting them.

A drug addict, for example, only needs to believe that they can quit, and they will be able to it. But how do you bridge that gap between knowledge and practice? How do you use the power of belief to change your life? This is the power of your mind at work.

Belief is nothing more than a set of rules that you use as your base programming to make sense of things (e.g., like how the world operates). When that drug addict is faced with the reality that his life needs to change, he finds a slot in an overall map of the world that he uses as a basis for reality. He sees the world is hard, which sets addicts up for failure.

As a result, the addict will constantly fail unless their belief system changes. It means getting out there and challenging beliefs and understanding that people do recover and lives do change. It means rejecting negative thoughts about addicts. It means embracing the willpower to change his life.

Limiting beliefs will always hold you back from achieving your life goals. If you have not been able to break through in a certain area of your life, it could be because your belief system is holding you back. The good news is that all beliefs can be influenced using your thoughts.

Remember that wellbeing[98] is abundantly available to you, but your thoughts matter. Training your thoughts to adopt a specific perspective can help you alter your belief system. Affirmations are one method of doing this, and they involve combating negative thoughts when they happen and replacing them with positive ones instead.

- Recognize that your belief system needs to change.
- Combat negative thoughts that reinforce this belief system.
- Actively and consciously replace them with positive thoughts.
- Repeat affirmations to yourself 5-10 times daily.
- Decide to believe in your new, chosen system.
- Practical Strategies: Becoming a Goal Master

Goal setting is a habit that will help you through every step of life, and it will help your mind make sense of those knowledge "gaps" that need to be translated into action. Goals are the driving force behind the plans that you put in place for your life.

To set a goal, establish a clear internal image of what you desire. Act as if the thing you want is right in front of you. Let it fill you up, and bask in the glow of what could be. Now you are going to translate this experience, feeling, and set of thoughts into a practical goal.

There are five main rules that you need to remember when achieving goals:

- You need to state the outcome in a positive manner. Be positive!

---

98   Mind Power – How to Break Free of Limiting Beliefs, http://www.wellbeingalignment.com/mind-power.html

- You need to be extremely specific and super detailed. Use your five senses.
- You need to have evidence of the procedure. Are you close or far away from it?
- You need to be with cause. Are you in control of attaining this goal?
- You need to verify that the outcome is ecologically sound and desirable. Does it support universal laws and the rights of your fellow man?

If all of these rules are covered, then they will be in line with the goals that you set. From this point, you can use the traditional goal setting method known as the SMART goal.

SMART[99] involves the structure involved in setting your goal. Using language, we create a goal that is not only achievable but feasible too. SMART stands for Specific, Measurable, Attainable, Relevant, and Time Sensitive.

All of your goals need to be well defined; easy to measure with rewards, numbers, dates, and schedules; attainable in your current reality; relevant to what you want to achieve in your life; and set to a specific timeline. A good goal might be "to learn French by the 10th of December, focusing on different aspects of the language each month"; a bad goal would be "to learn French this year."

You can become a goal master as you set SMART goals in your life to get ahead. People that set goals achieve more in their average week than most other people, so adopt this habit! It will help you achieve success in your life.

Practical Strategies: The Eternal Optimist

One of the most amazing powers that you have as a human being is your influence over your thoughts. You have complete control over

---

99 Golden Rules of Goal Setting, http://www.mindtools.com/pages/article/newHTE_90.htm

what you think at all times. I can tell you from personal study that any plan or conviction of purpose that is backed by a state of mind called faith is taken by the unconscious mind and manifested quickly.

We are the only members of the animal kingdom capable of controlling our emotions and thoughts internally. It is essential to change our habits of emotional response by combining reason with action. In other words, you feel the emotion—then you use your thoughts to make sense of it so that you can decide the right course of action.

This skill will keep you as an eternal optimist, which is a very desirable trait to have as a human being. Our attitude is the most important ingredient to achieving any successful outcomes we desire. In addition, attitude towards others determines their attitude towards us.

You must think, act, and talk like the person you want to become... right now. Not tomorrow, not 10 weeks from now, but today. Your present reality is all that you have. You need to adopt the traits of the person you wish to be and practice them daily.

That is why as an optimist,[100] you will remember to have gratitude for everything you are given and everything you give. When you speak, you will refer to positive life experiences to lift people up and not tear them down. You will forgive easily and authentically and work on becoming a better listener by actually listening instead of waiting for your turn to talk.

Focus on smiling more and frowning less, get lots of sunlight as part of your daily routine, exercise, eat well, and make a point of being helpful and nice to people. Optimists do not need a reason to embrace life; they simply do it every day.

When obstacles arise, choose to see them as a challenge and face them with a positive attitude. Motivate yourself however you can—

---

100 Remez Sasson, How to Be Optimistic, http://www.successconsciousness.com/how-to-be-optimistic.htm

with books, quotes, and TV shows. Take pride in how you dress; the better you look, the better you will feel. And always remember that happiness starts from within and works its way out.

Practical Strategies: Resourceful Visioning

Another excellent strategy for learning how to control your mind is called resourceful visioning. All thoughts, whether they are positive or negative, attract the people and things that are akin to it. In other words, your brain is a giant receiver and broadcasting transmitter for your thoughts and intentions.

Look at it this way: all internal cobwebs are spun by a negative mental attitude, the strongest of which are apathy and inactivity. These internal states of mind lead to ignorance and a closed mind! You have to be highly aware of what you are broadcasting to the world.

Your state of mind is like a siren song calling out to other people who feel the same way as you do; it can either attract or repel them. If you go out in a negative frame of mind and are relentlessly negative about everything, you will only attract other negative people into your life.

That is why you need an arsenal of resourceful states. You need to alter your emotions. If you feel yourself slipping, use thoughts, breathing patterns, and mental imagery to place yourself in a more favorable mental state.

Some states[101] make you feel confident, others relaxed or happy. Get to know what kind of images influence each state, and store them in your memory bank. Then create affirmations to help you overcome the negative thoughts you experience. A stressed person going to a party, for example, might excuse themselves and correct their mindset.

---

101 Rahul Rox, Invoking Resourceful States, http://voice2vision.net/invoking-resourceful-states/

Using resourceful visioning, they will take five minutes to calm down then breathe and focus on positive images of nature—a calm waterfall, a crackling fire, a verdant forest. They will then repeat distressing affirmations to themselves to realign their thoughts. "I have left my stress at home. I feel refreshed, energized, and confident...."

Any human being in the world has the power to instantly change their mindset with resourceful visioning. The best part is that once you are being more friendly and positive, the people around you will feel the same again. You will attract more positive people to you!

Practical Strategies: The Mirror Concept

Have you ever heard of the mirror concept in life? Reality is a mirror image of your expectations. If you think about this, you begin to realize that perhaps you have set your expectations a little low.

Everyone in the world has expectations about themselves, other people, the world, and even upcoming events. These expectations alter your view of the world more than you think. Most often these expectations are for the worse and are doing damage to your perception.

Here is a scenario that puts this concept into practice. You tell a friend about a new movie. When you hype it up because you enjoyed it, it creates unrealistic expectations for your friend. Then when they see the movie, they are viewing it through skeptical eyes. They want to see what made it so "good" for you. As a result, they may not enjoy the movie as much.

So expectations[102] can have a negative impact on how you see things. It also works with many of our other five senses, food in particular! When you expect a specific taste at a restaurant and you do not get it, it does not matter what the new taste is—nine people out

---

102 Thorin Klosowski, How Your Expectations Mess With Your View of the Present, http://lifehacker.com/how-your-expectations-mess-with-your-view-of-the-presen-1685353419

of ten will not like the new taste! This all boils down to expectations, those little preconceived notions we use to judge the world around us.

For this reason, I want you to keep the mirror concept in mind as you go through life. Reality is just a mirror of your expectations. In some areas, you can change this for the better, and you should. Expect to look nice every day. Expect to be happy, to succeed, and to treat people with respect every day.

But watch out for those notions that make you skeptical and transform all of your experiences into negative ones. Never listen to hype, and experience things for yourself as you see them. Do not allow other people's opinions to carry so much weight that you cannot make up your own mind about something.

The mirror concept will help you build a world around you that you want. It matters, so do not be afraid to make a physical impact where it is needed.

CHAPTER 13

FACT #4: ABSORBING INTERPERSONAL CONNECTION

"When it comes to developing character strength, inner security and unique personal and interpersonal talents and skills in a child, no institution can or ever will compare with, or effectively substitute for, the home's potential for positive influence."

Stephen Covey

Interpersonal connection is one of the most fundamental parts of what makes us human. People need people for love, validation, learning, and life. You cannot be considered a balanced human being if you avoid people or dislike being around them.

While it is true that there are introverts and extroverts, the fact remains that no one can be successful in life without strong human connections. This chapter will teach you how to get the most out of your social bonds so that you can live a healthy, balanced life.

The Catastrophic Impact of Holding onto Social Baggage

We all have social baggage that has caused scars from various past relationships. But allowing these to grow inside you so that they prevent or limit future relationships is where the trouble comes in.

This can have a catastrophic impact on your social life and result in feelings of isolation, loneliness, and alienation. In many cases, if left unresolved, social phobias and social anxiety can severely restrict your growth and interpersonal connections.

When around people, you are more likely to experience negative emotions like fear, apprehension, avoidance, pain, and anxiety. You become terrified of rejection and start to avoid meeting new people. Then you begin to stop seeing people that you love: your friends and family members.

Eventually, social dysfunction leaves you longing for human engagement and completely unable to enjoy it. Social anxiety disorder is the third largest[103] psychological problem in the United States. Clearly, people want to connect, but their own social baggage prevents it.

Do not allow yourself to hang onto social avoidant behaviors. Seek out solutions, and I do not mean taking a pill for it. Face your fears, and try to courageously confront your unwillingness to be judged by people. Human beings are social creatures that require the interpersonal connection.

Parental and Generational Mistakes: Forgiveness

The world is hard, but even harder than the world is raising kids when you barely have a grip on who you are. And that is why you need to release the negative feelings that you have for your parents and the mistakes they made when you were growing up.

---

103 Thomas A. Richards, Ph.D., What Is It Like to Live With Social Anxiety?, https://socialanxietyinstitute.org/living-with-social-anxiety

Forgiveness is the most healing of all the emotions. You need to stop hanging[104] onto the past and what happened in your home when you were growing up and forgive the troubles, mistakes, and bad experiences that you had with your parents.

Parents are people too. They are trying to make their way through the world and find their place, just like you are. No one is perfect—but that does not mean that they deserve to be blamed. When you get older and your parents become much older, it is time for reconciliation.

You cannot fully appreciate the struggles that your parents went through or the choices they made. You have to trust that they did the best they could with the resources they were given—even if a lot of the time it did not seem like enough. I am not speaking about forgetting but rather about letting go of the toxic emotions that have been carried for too many years

Parents are blamed but not trained! Stop judging them; times were different, and there was less information around. Spend time with your parents redefining your relationship so that it will work again.

Be grateful[105] that you learned how not to raise your kids in some aspects, and forgive your parents for being all they knew how to be. Self-introspection and clinical guidance regarding one's family of origin and their particular "family dance" is crucial to prevent similar parental sleepwalking from entering into the next generation. Understand that your parents are likely just products of their own parents' mistakes and flaws. Write it all down, and burn the letter if you have to.

Learn from your parents' strengths and their weaknesses, and count them all as blessings. Remember always, as has been stated

104 Veronica Nguyen, Learning to Forgive Our Imperfect Parents for Their Mistakes, http://tinybuddha.com/blog/learning-to-forgive-our-imperfect-parents-for-their-mistakes/
105 Ken Wert, 12 Ways to Forgive Your Parents for Doing Such a Crummy Job of Raising You, http://www.stevenaitchison.co.uk/blog/12-ways-to-forgive-your-parents/

numerous times in this book, adversity can be seen as a karmic gift created to empower you with new, invaluable life insights and lessons. Allow the way that you communicate with your own children to be the healing salve that soothes your spirit. Always take responsibility for how your life is, and display compassion to all.

Stepping Away From Toxic Relationships

You know the loving saying "you complete me"? There is an opposite saying, "you deplete me," and this happens when you have toxic relationships in your life. They are easy to spot, and I bet a few have just floated into your mind right now.

A relationship does not have to be romantic to be toxic. It can exist in your friendship group or in your close family. It can even exist at work, although these relationships are a little trickier to navigate. A relationship becomes toxic when there is no give and take, only take, take, take. When another human being leaves you feeling sad, depressed, or angry after every encounter, they are unhealthy people to be around.

When you are with that person[106] and you can never do anything right no matter how hard you try, it is toxic. When everything is about them and never about you, it is toxic. And when things have become so bad that you cannot even enjoy the good moments with that person, the relationship is toxic. You need to cut it out of your life.

Ending a toxic relationship can be very hard. But you need to step out of denial. If this person is constantly making you feel terrible, they should not be in your life. To convince yourself of it, keep a log of your emotions. How does this person make you feel on a day-to-day basis? It is easy to ignore an experience and not so easy to ignore 30 days of it.

---

106 Yvette Bowlin, 5 Signs You're in a Toxic Relationship, http://tinybuddha.com/blog/5-signs-youre-in-a-toxic-relationship/

Identify the perks[107] of the toxic relationship, and weigh up if they are worth the sacrifice you are making. Can you get these perks somewhere else? If so, fill that hole or make a plan to bridge that gap. Then surround yourself with positive friends and people, and it will get easier. Soon you will find that you do not miss that horrible drain on your spirit.

Practical Strategies: Reciprocal Happiness

The only relationships that you need to nurture in your life are the ones that provide you with reciprocal happiness. This is a term that means when you are with these people, they fill a social or emotional need for you that is positive, and you do the same for them.

Of course there will be bad days, but largely, your relationships should be positive. It should not be a relationship where one person simply complains to the other about things all the time. Sharing joy, dreams, and plans is a vital part of making them come true.

When someone does this with you, it means that they care and want to share their life with you. Otherwise relationships can become terribly limited. Remember that when you communicate with someone else, you must refrain from processing your innermost emotions in excessive detail because that only causes them to over attach to your pain.

What you are looking for is empathy, not sympathy. One is dysfunctional, and the other is healing. Always consider the person you are with, and speak to them as if you respect their emotional energy as much as your own. By all means, share if you need to, but be mindful of doing this too often in case you become a drain on your friends and family.

Reciprocal happiness is a beautiful thing. In relationships where you have this bond, you will look upon engagement with excitement

---

107 Therese J. Borchard, You Deplete Me: 10 Steps to End a Toxic Relationship, http://psychcentral.com/blog/archives/2010/03/15/you-deplete-me-10-steps-to-end-a-toxic-relationship/

and joy. Spending time with these people is satisfying and elating, and it energizes you.

To find these relationships in life, you have to be clear about your emotional boundaries and needs. When someone dumps on you, listen, but then remember to withdraw your emotions and protect yourself. Make it your mission to improve the day of every person you meet, and soon you will have more friends than you can manage.

Practical Strategies: Unconscious Communication

Communication comes in many different formats, and socially speaking, the most important of these is not speech! Each person communicates on a conscious level with words, but they also communicate on an unconscious level using their tone of voice, rate of speech, and physical body; breathing patterns, posture, gestures,[108] and eye movements are all involved.

To accomplish anything in life, you need to be able to communicate effectively. Whether it is the kind of relationship that you want to attract or a spiritual or financial goal, communication is always the key to making it happen.

People connect with others very easily. When these connections happen and an individual feels like they have bonded with you, it is called "rapport." The most important process in any interaction is rapport. When it is missing, you notice it is not there.

At best, the average person uses their skills with rapport randomly and unconsciously. But by acquiring new skills and focusing on the process, you can also learn how to increase effective communication between you and others.

Unconscious communication like voice tone, gestures, and breathing patterns should all be matched with the person you are

---

108 Use Body Language to Build Rapport, http://www.businessweek.com/smallbiz/tips/ archives/2010/11/use_body_language_to_build_rapport.html

talking to. This helps put people at ease and quickly establishes a rapport with them.

You need to learn to listen with your eyes, heart, and ears. Just your ears is not good enough! Only 7% of communication is contained in words; the rest comes from body language (55%) and how we say those words—or the tone and feeling reflected in our voice (38%). This is where the real power of rapport lies.

Practical Strategies: Establishing Rapport

What are the most effective methods of establishing rapport with other people, you may ask? Most effective rapport is established in a non-verbal sense, so you will not have to remember to say anything witty to get it right.

There are three main ways to quickly and easily establish rapport with someone new:

1. *Match their tone of voice or their tempo.* This means being in tune with how they sound and the emotions they are conveying. Is their pitch high or low? Loud or soft? How fast are they talking, and can you match it? Speak just like you hear them speak to you.

2. *Focus on matching their breathing rate.* Breathe with them to put them at ease. Focus on getting the speed right, and breathe from the area of the body they are breathing from. It takes practice, but you can get it right.

3. *People subconsciously like people that look like them.* Try to match their physiology and not be self-conscious. Focus on mirroring their gestures, body posture, eye blink rate, and facial muscle movements. You do this naturally when you are in sync with someone.

Remember that this process is subtle, so do not announce that you are doing it, or it may scare off the person you are talking to. Words are only a small percentage of what makes us great communicators, so do not be afraid to delve into the world of physiology and find out what body language can do for your communication skills.

Here is a challenge. Tonight find someone you know, and listen to them speak. Try mirroring their actions in a subtle way, and notice how much it pleases them. You may even get compliments for being so in tune with them!

Practical Strategies: Relationship Affinity

Interpersonal skills are also extremely important when it comes to dealing with conflict scenarios. Use the relationship affinity technique to control yourself the next time trouble brews and you feel yourself spiraling into a fight with someone.

When this interpersonal conflict arises, do not place blame. Start with yourself first. Make a point of being more flexible than your partner—not a "yes" person but more flexible within reason. Make a point of listening with patience to sincerely understand their point of view.

Ask yourself—do I really believe what I have just said? Or did I make it up on the spot because I want to be right or because I do not understand what is happening? Always respond to your significant other with respect and kindness.

Ultimate control is always in the hands of the person who is the most flexible. You have the power to end every fight that begins if you listen without judgment and with a critical ear. Being flexible in a relationship means actively considering the other person's feelings and placing them above your own to a certain extent.

This should never compromise your own emotions, but it should lead to faster resolutions when fights do break out. When you can settle fights this way—logically and in a caring manner—it will create relationship affinity between you and the other person.

As the saying goes, learn how to bend so that you do not break! Too many relationships break over silly reasons of pride, stubbornness, and purely selfish feelings. Think of the last few fights that you have had with someone—was there a point? Or was it simply the transfer of negative emotions like frustration? How could you have solved it?

Practical Strategies: Words Shape Others

Your words have the ability to shape other people; you can either lift them up or tear them down. You may not even be aware that you are doing these things with your words. That is why it is important that you are consciously aware of what you say to people and how you say it. Otherwise you may be causing damage!

The quality of a person's[109] life depends on the quality of their communication. We use speech patterns to help communicate with others in a more mindful, conscious manner rather than just talking recklessly at each other, sparing no one's feelings.

Try to understand the other person's point of view first. Do not expect them to understand your point of view before you do.

As a rule, only speak about people who are present to keep the exchange meaningful and positive.

Often it is not what you say but how it is said that matters. You communicate more with your energy, emotions, gestures, and body language than you do with words. Take note of how the other person is feeling, and elevate their spirit as needed.

Be still within yourself, listen to others, and speak kindly so that you do not injure them.

The meaning of any communication is the response that it gets from the other human being. If it elicits anger, you have done something wrong. Accept responsibility for that and recover. Never expect other people to take something the way you meant it. Insisting on that is not good communication; it is shirking responsibility.

---

109 Julie Miller, Being Consciously Aware of Your Speech, http://lightworkers.org/channeling/193676/being-consciously-aware-your-speech

Effective communicators are not individuals with good command of the English language. In fact, they are individuals who are dialed into other people—the way they feel. Having sensory acuity and behavioral flexibility will make you high in demand during any social gathering.

CHAPTER 14
FACT #5: EMBRACE SPIRITUAL ALIGNMENT

"The problem with the chemical route to God is that the drug user seeks to short circuit that whole demanding process, analogous to the small child awestruck by the circus & longs to see it but is unwilling to earn the price of admission. One cannot simply sneak into the Kingdom of God."
Alan Cohen

Spiritual alignment is a worthy cause to seek out during your lifetime. Our spiritual sides have been repressed for far too long. I believe if people were more in touch with their spirits, they would know more about their place in the world.

That is why this final chapter is going to teach you strategies on renewing and reigniting your spiritual side. When your spirit is in line with the rest of your domains, incredible things happen. This is when leading a successful life is not only probable but highly likely.

The Modern Tragedy of Spirit

Society is consumed with material success, and as a result, we have all missed out on a fundamental truth—that success depends on who you are, not what you do or what you have. Your "spirit" or "being" is at the source of all achievement in life.

Because the spirit is quite an abstract notion, people have never regarded it as a particularly useful thing. The irony, of course, is that even the oldest traditions of human wisdom mention fixed, knowable, and reliable principles that involve the human spirit.

The spirit may be silent, but it can be woken up. It does not relate to religion but is rather a broad concept of your internal self. This is what has been lost today, and this is our modern tragedy. Spirituality[110] is many things:

- It unites you and me, regardless of culture, race, or religion.
- It is involved with trust, forgiveness, and a zest for life.
- It means love, commitment, inner longing, and nonmaterial reality.
- It is the path to discovering one's true purpose in life.
- It is personal, individual, and subjective.
- It is inward, hidden, and energized by deep personal longings.
- It is our capacity to relate to the infinite.

When you seize the opportunity to embrace spiritual alignment, you reactivate the part of yourself that knows exactly where you need to go and how you intend to get there.

Recognizing the Spirit within You

Spirituality is a deeply personal thing. It concerns your own first-hand connection with the infinite universe, and it reflects your own

---

110 Leslee J. Klinsky, Aligning With Your Higher Self, http://healing.about.com/od/higherself/a/alignhigherself.htm

spiritual experiences. These experiences are important, and they direct us to the deepest source of power that comes from recognizing our unity with the rest of all creation.

Many of us have had spiritual experiences in life—sudden inspiration, transcending personal limitations, feeling connected to nature or to people, and experiencing meaningful coincidences and synchronicities that happen. These leave us with a sense that we are being guided by a force beyond our own understanding.

Mystical experiences are happy too—like when we witness stunning art or music, have a near death experience, or experience a private moment of transcendent awareness. These involve personal experiences of realities that are beyond our ordinary or limited perception of who we are.

You need to learn to value your spiritual domain and to develop it so that it ranks of equal important to your mental, emotional, social, and physical development. Many spiritual experiences are stored in the subconscious mind as coincidence or serendipity.

They impact our lives, changing things beyond rational explanation, yet we dismiss them without special consideration. When we fail to validate our spiritual experiences, we deny their existence, which is not healthy.

Spiritual denial can be seen in how many people fail to realize that mental and physical balance are needed in life. It is the spirit that tells this to us. Those that lack conscious recognition of the spirit often report feeling that life is meaningless and lacks purpose.

So I want to encourage you to stop denying your spirit. When you do deny it, it pulls you into self-destructive behaviors, unhealthy relationships, and addictions. Free yourself of the idea that your spirit means nothing, because it is everything.

People that are in tune with their spirit know where to go in life, what their purpose is, and why they need to follow it. The spirit inside you wants to connect and help other people with your unique gifts, and it is time that you let it.

The Process of Spiritual Recovery: Begin Now

Today marks the first day of your spiritual recovery. The process transcends those that have been impacted by addictions. Complete recovery involves the full continuum of healing—from the biological and psychological to retrieving the spiritual dimensions of your existence.

The very definition of recovery needs to be expanded to include recovery from mental and emotional addictions, traits like self-sabotage, and behaviors like underachievement, self-deprecation, and negative projections of the self.

Recovery[111] comes from conscious and unconscious beliefs, attitudes, and behaviors that keep us from manifesting our true potential. People often complain about feeling a spiritual void, which is exactly what has happened to us in our modern lives. The spirit has been crowded out of existence to make room for material things.

As we know, material possessions might bring temporary pleasure yet never true, lasting fulfillment. Fulfillment makes people happy! With every life situation, there is another problem for us to solve in our own way. Taking responsibility for this is important. Human existence is therefore a process of self-transcendence rather than self-fulfillment.

When we are confronted with an inescapable situation—faced with a fate that we cannot change—we are given a last chance to transcend suffering by shifting our internal attitude. This is how suffering and pain cease. With positive meaning, anything can be improved. Life is difficult—there will be ups and downs—but that is what it means to be human.

You have to allow your spirit the room to evolve. This means that you need to prevail over any underlying tendency that you have to gain pleasure or avoid suffering in your life. You need to search to uncover the inherent value in your life.

---

111 Phil Fox Rose, What Works: Spiritual Recovery, http://bustedhalo.com/features/what-works-6-spiritual-recovery

Everyone needs to embrace the reality that you are consistently creating for yourself. Each choice sets a scene, and that has become your life. At any moment you must be aware that every choice you make concerns your spirit and your eventual goal of gaining a deeper life purpose and a higher spirituality.

Begin now. The next time you feel inspired, acknowledge your spirit. Hasten to get the ideas down. The next time you hear a song that plays and it fills your heart, listen. What is it trying to tell you? It is time to unleash the potential that has been hiding within.

Practical Strategies: You Are More Than Your Thoughts

I have already told you that you are more than your thoughts, but do you know how much more? Each of us is part of a much bigger, interactive system—one in which cause and effect cannot be isolated from its context. This system is made up of your mind, your body, and your eternal spirit. Every dimension must be measured in terms of the whole!

One of the most important things about our human existence is the capacity to rise above adverse situations and overcome them. You are so much more than those limited perceptions and are not merely a result of biological, social, and psychological conditions. Nor are you merely a product of heredity and your environment.

You are born incomplete, and you need to determine who you are. You decide whether to succumb to life's conditions or to challenge them and win. Your life is self-determined, my friend! Only you know what your existence will be.

Only you understand what you are in the next moment. All people have the freedom to change in less than an instant. A lot of people believe that a human energy field surrounds us and carries with it a lot of emotional energy created by internal and external experiences—positive and negative.

The human system carries past and current[112] relationships with

---

112 Frederic and Mary Ann Brussat, Harvesting Memories, http://www.

it, profound and traumatic experiences and memories, and all of our beliefs and attitudes. The emotions from these experiences have become coded into our biology and contribute to our formation of cell tissue, which in turn generates a quality of energy that reflects those past emotions.

Not everyone believes this in such a literal sense, but it is plausible. Past trauma and pain must be worked through and reframed as constructive suffering so that in the future, it can bring you joy if you want any chance of gaining positive meaning out of a worldly existence. Pain and disease are the universe's way of getting our attention.

Once the universe has our attention, we need to undergo a process of transformation in our lives. We have been invited to a higher form of thinking, and we should always accept that invitation. The first step lies in the desire to view your life's misfortunes in a different way.

Heal yourself by disciplining your mind to think of the past as a learning experience and gain joy from it. Then remain open to all future learning experiences.

Practical Strategies: Spiritual Balance & Health

Can your spirit[113] impact your health? Of course it can. Wellness and illness are way more complex than science has made them out to be. The impact of our existence rests solely in the meaning that we ascribe to the world around us. The meaning that you assign to your life events is directly linked with mind modulation of all body systems that influence your health.

In other words, the meaning you assign to your life either improves or degenerates your health. There is no separation between the

---

spiritualityandpractice.com/practices/features.php?id=17004

113 Claudia St. Claire, 21 Essential Tricks for Achieving Spiritual Balance in the Midst of Chaos, http://thoughtcatalog.com/claudia-st-clair/2014/02/21-essential-tricks-for-achieving-spiritual-balance-in-the-midst-of-chaos/

mental, emotional, physical, spiritual, and interpersonal domains in our lives, so we have to assume that wellness comes from expanding our awareness and personal potential.

Stated simply, it means that you need to learn to fully grasp the meaning you give to your life's experiences, because they matter. Stop denying your spiritual nature just because as a culture, you do not have any sanctioned frameworks in which to deeply experience and satisfy the yearning for wholeness that you innately desire!

If you have recognized your need for wholeness, well done. Many people will never even get that far. It is a journey that must be travelled. People that are unaware of their spiritual potential because they lack direct experience or necessary supporting beliefs, often define their lives as completely meaningless.

Due to these pervasive feelings of restlessness and a desire for something more, they act out. An unidentified yearning can cause severe self-destruction in an individual that does not understand it. This attracts self-destructive relationships and emotions, negative thinking, addictions, and all sorts of horrible adversity into their lives.

As a direct result, their health suffers! What would happen if you chose to use your agitated inner state to propel you towards spiritual possibility? Perhaps you could fulfill your soul's quest for wholeness and life purpose!

Learn to feed your soul like you feed your body. Meditation, prayer, serving others, reading, drawing, painting, thinking deeply, music, walking, and being with friends are all excellent ways of making sure that your spirit is being fed. This is turn will benefit you as you become healthier and happier in your pursuit to finding your life's ultimate purpose.

Practical Strategies: Spiritual Philosophy

Throughout history, mankind has recorded how important the spirit is to people. The message is always the same whether you are

Christian, Hindu, Buddhist, Jewish, or Islamic: "At the bottom of one's soul is the soul of humanity itself, a divine, transcendent soul, leading from bondage to liberation, from enchantment to awakening, from time to eternity, from death to immortality."[114]

Take a minute now to stop to consider the basic premise for all the major religions and spiritual philosophies in the world...

Buddhists believe that nothing is permanent, that the world and everyone in it are in constant change. The universe and everyone in it are connected, and the law of cause and effect is in play. Whatever you do comes back to you in some way. Buddha even means "the awakened one." The top rule? Hurt not others with that which pains yourself.

Christians believe in one God, a supreme being who created the universe and gave people rules for living a good life. God sent his only son, Jesus, to die for humanity's sins. Jesus taught people to love one another and to love God how God has loved you. He taught the world to forgive everyone, even their enemies. The top rule? Do unto others as you would have them do unto you.

Hindus believe that every person's spirit is a part of the great spirit of the universe called Brahman. It is eternal and everywhere, with no beginning and no end. Hindus teach non-violence, truthfulness, respect for parents and the elderly, simple living, and helping the needy. The top rule? Treat others as you yourself would be treated.

Islamic people believe in one God, the same God as the Jews and the Christians. Muslims must follow the five pillars of Islam: to believe in God, to pray, to give to those in need, to eat and drink nothing (from sunrise to sunset) during the month of Ramadan, and to take a pilgrimage to Mecca. The top rule? Do unto all men as you would wish to have done unto you.

Jews believe in one God who created the universe and everything in it. The top rule? What you yourself hate, do to no man. The same

---

114 Ken Wilber, No Boundary: Eastern and Western Approaches to Personal Growth.

can be said for Native American religions that revere nature. All creatures are a living example of one great spirit that is everywhere and in everything. The top rule is to live in harmony for we are all related.

Practical Strategies: Your Own Divine Energy

These days there is a contemporary spiritual perspective that has been called "a course in miracles," and it also relates to similar spiritual precepts that have withstood the test of time. This belief system says that everything that happens in our lives is an opportunity to heal and forgive something deep within us.

Some people believe that we are really spiritual beings merely living a temporary physical existence. We get spiritual information through our minds by way of dreams, insight, intuition, and our feelings. The eventual outcome is to have your life represent the expression of love that can only happen if you choose to hear the spirit rather than the ego.

All problems have solutions in healing through forgiveness. The more you can be still and let go of the ego to the extent that you hear more clearly whatever you need to know, the better. It should be your goal to become so healed within that your spirit speaks and acts through you.

Talking and seeing with your spirit's eyes is an attitude. It means being self-aware and noticing non-coincidences and miracles; they happen to help us shift our perspective and awaken us to the spirit within. Miracles should always inspire gratitude.

You must yearn to become more spiritually aware and aligned so that you can go back home to your creator at the end of your life. This quest can only be reached when you transcend your ego's illusion that you are separate from one another rather than connected. You do not need ego defenses like anger, hurt, and feelings of victimization.

You possess your own divine energy[115] that wants to shine out from within you. It is your soul's quest to recognize that the "kingdom of God" is inside you. You only need to remember that you are a divine spirit trying to return home. You can enter the kingdom by integrating your divinity with your humanity.

Surrender your ego and desire for control, and expand your consciousness. So much research has been done on the mind–body–soul connection. You must begin to believe that what you believe is true! If you believe you can, you are right! So never believe that you cannot, and it will never be.

Practical Strategies: Presence and Passion

"Don't ask yourself what the world needs. Ask yourself what makes you come alive and then go do that. Because what the world needs is people who have come alive."
Howard Thurman

You need to discover the quest of your soul. You possess unique talents and a responsibility to contribute to the world in a manner that no one else can. Deep down inside, you know this to be true. Life calls you to awaken to your spiritual dimension as you discover these unique skills and talents that will help you fulfill your soul's quest for a meaningful and purposeful life.

Just by being aware of your specifically unique talents, you can begin to design a personal vision or mission for yourself. This will be a beacon to guide you during times of uncertainty and despair. You need to learn how to live your life backwards in time.

This means consulting your future vision constantly and having it motivate your life based on what could be rather than what fear of the past you have internalized. When you are confronted with these

---

115 Spiritual Enlightening – Reception of the Divine Energy, http://www.trivedieffect.com/spiritual-enlightening-reception-of-the-divine-energy/

FEARs (False Evidence Appearing Real), remember that they are transitory in nature, and the truth of your life lies in a higher vision.

You will need courage to move ahead in spite of your fear! Invest more into your visions of the future rather than your accepted view of reality, and you will be blessed. Your spirit's plan for you is to discover your true self while experiencing joy, even through unsettling times. When your life feels out of control, you must look within.

You can be guided by the all-knowing wisdom of the ages if you allow it. You must be willing to abandon your mistakes and your wrong beliefs because it is not possible to steer your spiritual path by way of the ego. You must surrender and be guided by forces in your life that are beyond your control.

When you allow this spiritual force to guide you, your life will be truly unique. You cannot get into heaven wearing someone else's costume! Your greatest strength will come in expressing your unique gifts. There is no greater gift than to offer those who have forgotten a glimpse at what life could be like if only they acknowledged their spirit.

Here are four traits of people who express their unique personal missions every day:

1. *They are passionate.* They love what they do even when it gets rough.
2. *They are talented.* They are very good at what they do; they have the gift!
3. *They find value in it.* Doing what they do is very important to them.
4. *They have a sense of destiny.* They were born to do what they are doing.

CONCLUSION
BE YOU

"To awaken the miraculous unfolding of the Spirit within us all, while supporting individuals to make a positive difference in each other's lives; thereby maximizing our God-given potential and fulfilling our soul's quest for purpose."

Mark Armiento's Personal Mission

What if you could manifest your positive intentions, break free of self-limiting dialogue, release yourself from negative emotions, and live a happier, healthier life? Hopefully, by now you have a clear path forward—a path that will lead to a more fulfilled you.

And all you have to do is...be you. The world tries to mold you into many things, and this is where we go wrong. It is not enough to live just to survive; you have to live according to your purpose, your passion. You have to find your place in this world!

You are an explorer; you have simply forgotten to explore. A great life means taking some great risks, but if you allow yourself to remain balanced in your pursuit, it will be easier. Life balance gives you an advantage like no other I have ever seen.

I have watched as ruined people have transformed themselves into luminaries. I have seen the impact that balance can have on a single life. Life is a series of lessons preparing you for something great. Adversity helps you learn, and learn you must!

Becoming who you are would not be possible without challenges. Embrace them, and embrace the idea that you are more than your current reality. Anything is possible, it is true, but for you, very specific things are possible. It is your life journey to figure out what those things are and to bring your unique talents to the world.

This is when you will find love, acceptance, fulfillment, and real happiness. People do not know what is good for them, but trust your spirit, and it will guide you. Do not allow the extraordinary to go unnoticed, and do not allow your life to go by wasted.

You are able to open your arms to change and to transform the way that you have been thinking and feeling for all of this time. This is your wakeup call! No more sleepwalking on a tightrope or falling into the same traps over and over again.

It is time to forge a new path, hang a new wire, and venture—fully balanced—down that line towards greatness and eternity. You have the potential inside you; you just need to unleash it. Get out there, and make your life happen.

Eyes wide open—awaken to the spirit within!

Mark Armiento

Looking forward to hearing about your awakening at:
markarmiento.com

PRAISE FOR
MARK ARMIENTO

"The Gift of Mr. Armiento – I can express the extreme gratitude of such presence of Mr. Armiento but it doesn't express totally the unwavering gift of having him in your life and experiencing the changes that not only he is a supportive host of but the genuine backbone when it comes to understanding, and hearing your voice. He helps you move through your fears and pushes your strengths like a beautiful symphony. He teaches you to shine your light as a star on a dark night. He won't give up on you and surely under his watch won't allow you to give up on yourself. His wealth of information in not only empowering but also inspiring. If you grant him your ears he will guide you in seeing how life should appear. He is like a shower washing away all your insecurities making you even better for a new presentation of you and a more positive outlook on your future. You never have to guess if he is there because the reflection of his work is represented seeing yourself arrive in the driver seat of your life. He is your coach, your support system, a friend and one of your cheering fans. He takes his work seriously and will not leave you and will be a encore with you in your life's performance toward the greatest show ever. Having him in your life will be a memory you will never forget."

Shenetta Iese

"I'm a 64-year-old African-American grandmother, fulfilling a 10-year-old dream, once lost but now awakens as a direct result of the Mr. Armiento's school. During his classroom lectures he spoke to me about self -discovery through using gentle humor, allowing me not to take life so serious- in the search for "Waldo". He would smile while looking deep into my eyes, seeing my soul and replying: " you'll be introduced to the real Waldo soon". Mr. Armiento has awakened my spirit, once deferred. Words cannot express endless joy that I have discovered in learning about me (a.k.a. 'Waldo') "

Laurette R.

"Thank you for the everlasting gift you presented for all of us in class, Mr. Armiento. There was so much emotions and passion coming through me in every moment in the class. I guess what I am saying is that I felt every chakra and matter inside me vibrating and it would not stop. There were times I wanted to explode but I held it in. There were so many things you were hitting inside of me that I am ready to release and so many purposeful things that I am feeling that calling for me not to resist anymore. You say huge things in such simplicity that heals a person the moment they allow it to be fed into their minds. I am not trying to put you on a pedestal or anything just sharing what you have invoked inside of me....Now I no longer feel the need to save others- Nor do I feel opted to be their hero. I just could not see any of that before Mr. Armiento, I so appreciate you that it is making tears coming through my eyes. .... When I see you Mr. Armiento you are like a huge ocean that magnetizes and purges humanity in authenticities. Thank you soooo much. My arms go around you with so much gratitude. Man Mr. Armiento you are a store house of GOD Power."

Michelle W.

"Mark was a great Vice President at the Outreach Training for counselors for substance abuse. He inspired so many people in this program because of the special way that he connected with people. This program was one of the best run training programs that I have experienced and I am sure that the knowledge and personal attributes that made this program top notch also make Mark a great counselor. Many people told about how the program had changed their lives and I am sure he is continuing to help people change their lives as a counselor."

John B. W.

"My name is Eric, I'm 47 years old. I believed my life's better years were behind me, then I met Mark Armiento. My experience with this gentle man was life altering. His sense of self and purpose of helping others touched me, and awoken in me a belief how we are all connected in our pursuit of spirituality. His influence inspired me to become someone I was not aware of. I, today feel a freedom I cannot repay, Mark is a beautiful soul, a well-educated professional, and most importantly, a true human being. I am very grateful to have been brought into his hope for humanity, His solution based ideas for addressing behavioral issues profoundly changed my life forever. I feel he would become a valuable asset to any environment which involves him."

Eric R.

"Mark I just wanted to say that you're an amazing person and I admire and respect the work that you do. You have truly changed my life and the way that I think and for that I am grateful. I promise to spread the consciousness. I have finally found balance and peace with myself and became a human being not a human doing. Know that you are blessed"

Eddie P.

"I am not one who is easily impressed but Mark immediately got my attention! I was told by other students that I would love him because he has a great sense of humor, very knowledgeable and vibrates on a level that is not the norm- he thinks outside the box! Mark presents with such enthusiasm and passion, a great skill in and of itself. Mark vibrates on a level to where he is magnetic and you can't help but gravitate toward him. He exudes energy and confidence! If everything in life is energy his energy centers are lined and are lit up! Whomever crosses Mark's path consider yourself lucky. I am! Thank you, Mark for the role you have played in my life in such a short amount of time- You are a gift to so many!"

Aima D.

"The first time meeting Mr. Armiento I was immediately drawn to him. The day he lectured on Spirituality I received my "ah-ha" moment. Mr. Armiento is a great teacher with a Spirit that draws people -His awareness of self & spirit allowed me to open up and explore more of myself. I feel anyone would be blessed to have him in their lives, whether as a teacher, husband, father, therapist or friend. Mr. Armiento has a Dalai Lama spirit!

Latoya S.

"Mark opened up my eyes with the concept that I am making choice based on past hurts, past experiences and therefore, repeating negative life patterns. Mark showed me that I did not have to be a slave to my thoughts, that I could change my perception and life a positive, focused healthy life if I allowed myself to. I'm eating to live and be healthy. I exercise regularly. I feel great and I am changing my person choices not only in food but in how I approach relationships and even my marriage. Thank you for clearing the fog from my thoughts. I really love the classes you teach and the Life Balance Advantage you gave so freely."

Lisa L.

"I will never be able to express how Mark has impacted my life! Mark, I thank you so much. I have changed my life so dramatically. I literally did a 360. As a man/mentor, I admire you and look up to you. As a teacher, you have installed that yearning to learn more. My mind, body, and soul has been awakened!"

Jonathan B.

"What I have achieved has changed my life. I will never be the same! My changes are not cosmetic, rather they are rooted in my soul. I am so thankful to you Mark. Nothing has awoken me more than what I have learned during our time together. How do you thank a person for helping you not only get back your life, but helping you find a meaningful one? I will honor and thank you by living a life that exemplifies what I have learned."

Gwenne L.

"In his teachings, I learned to value my life and to believe that hope was for everyone. Mark brings to the broken, the realization that cultivating kindness promotes acceptance, peace, freedom and happiness. Marks shows us that we can learn to be spiritual, we can learn to pay attention in the present moment and more importantly, we can change our habitual patterns our vulnerabilities to automatic reactions based on past experiences of hurt. Mark shows us that too often we're on auto pilot, not even paying attention to what is actually happening in in the present, just responding to triggers that cause us to react automatically and defensively respond. The way Mark presents, it allows one to engage more fully with ones emotions and experiences. He shows us the infinite possibilities if we allow ourselves to hear and forgive and move forward without judgement for past actions that cannot be changed. I am forever indebted to Mark Armiento for the light he shed on my life and empowerment received from his message."

Kristina J. D.

"Mark changed my life!! He is an amazing spiritual force - mentor - guide. There wasn't a lecture where I didn't leave class teary eyed. I hope that I can carry his message out into the field. His lectures on Life Balance Advantage changed my life. He helped me find WALDO. Mark is a special person and I hope that you can in some special way recognize him for the gift he gave me and my peers at his training Institute."

Mr. Merritt H.

"I believe that Mark Armiento unveils the value of spirituality in recovery, which should become the model and primary focus for treatment modalities servicing persons seeking freedom from addictive behaviors. Mark proves that over time, with the right mind set and a belief that there is more, people do transform their lives permanently. I have seen and experienced personally a transformation in my own perception about life and my ability to really achieve my goals after being exposed to Mark and his Spirituality lectures. My classmates have all expressed inspirational transformation and perception changes because of Marks message of spirituality-they now look at their clients differently! Mark's teachings about Spirituality in Recovery make it easy for people like myself, to shout to the world, "This is it!"- Here is where you can find the answers to questions you've been asking all your life - Here is where you can find the first day of the rest of your life. The hope in Mark's selflessness equips students with a message that brings light to a world of darkness and instructs future therapists to help people find their true selves and achieve their life's potential."

Janet L.

"It's really amazing when I think about the positive impact you have had on SO MANY people. Do you ever think about that? You are truly blessed and are an inspiration for many. I hope that you never lose sight of that. By the way, I also thank you for your light in my life. You

HAVE made a difference! I like to tell people what they mean to me while they are alive; in my opinion, that's when it matters most. We may not cross paths frequently, but you have left an imprint inside of me that can't be erased. Shine on!"

Roy R.

"I actually called Mark a Jedi Knight on my evaluation. Everything about him is simply amazing; his knowledge is ridiculous. The way he hypnotizes this room seriously touches me. I could go on forever, but let's face it: I could sum it all up with one word, and that word is inspired!"

Ken C.

"Everyone has the realization that the things that have been in one's life are just not right or those things just don't work anymore. My personal journey with Mark happened this past year and it was one that I wished happened much sooner. But sometimes you just don't realize the tremendous pain that you are in until the pain slowly passes and you get that ultimate epiphany of self-awareness only to ask yourself, "Why did you put up with all that?" But you soon realize such because you found a compassionate and empathetic individual such as Mark who enables you to process that pain, direct it to an inner peace where you can safely express that pain, and then ultimately have the voice to continue working on yourself to be whom you have always meant to be. While I have been going through a tumultuous divorce and having my children who have had their own personal issues of their own, Mark has exhibited the grace of unwavering faith and trust as no other person that I have ever met. His guidance, knowledge, and commitment to helping me and my family have been incredulous and miraculous. He has an innate ability to help you discover the cause of your unhappiness and while you may think it is insurmountable, you find that peace and happiness that you have been searching for and the reason that you went to see him in the first place. God has blessed Mark with this ability. Although, I often call Mark and describe Mark as my "guru", I am truly blessed to call him my friend."

Patty C. Family

"Almost 20 years ago, a shy, insecure, insanely pained 19 year old embarked on a journey that would absolutely CHANGE my life. I was scared out of my mind but was encouraged by so many to take the leap of faith and go on Mark's retreat to "find my soul". And boy did I! I left my house angry, resentful, hurt, feeling unworthy and insignificant-and returned a completely different woman. The Soul Quest retreat was the turning point to my life's healing and recovery."

Robin Lynn

"My personal journey with Mark began in December at a time when I knew that a change was needed. My life was going through many difficult choices and obstacles and I needed someone to help direct me on a path that was challenging and to face the reasons why these obstacles were preventing me from having a fulfilling and peaceful life. As I struggled with a pending divorce and trying to raise children with difficult issues of their own, Mark had the grace of faith, trust and support like no other individual that I have ever known before. It is my belief that God has blessed Mark with these gifts because it is innate and comes so naturally to him and for me, the peace that I have wanted to achieve is coming into a life which has been stagnant for quite some time. In addition, to my own personal pain and issues, Mark has helped my own son, through his own issues with substance abuse and the realization of his own pain and the self-sabotage which he now is facing and trying to make amends and in which only a compassionate, empathetic and patient individual such as Mark can do. He has the incredible ability to make you process your pain, find your voice to express that pain, and then through his guidance help you find the "path" that you need to seek and need to focus on. I certainly am in gratitude for the tremendous support, faith, and trust that Mark has done for myself and my family. I often call and describe him as my "guru" because he is exactly that. I feel blessed that Mark has been an unwavering force in mine and my children's lives."

Patty Testani

"From the moment I met Mark, I knew I met someone special. I've worked with many therapists over the past ten years, each of whom have taught me something valuable about how certain events in my childhood may relate to who I have become today. Mark, on the other hand, lends a different approach to self-discovery and Life balance. He focuses more on what is going on in the PRESENT and offers realistic strategies to conquer challenges. He does not dismiss the past as an important part of you, nor does he ignore the future as an opportunity to reach your goals; but more importantly, he teaches you to stay centered and calm on what is going on in life as it is happening. Mark is a gifted healer who listens, offers sage advice and truly cares about your well-being."

Andrea Cohen, Westchester County, NY

"Meeting Mark Armiento at one of his "Life Balance Workshops" at St. John's University was by far one of the best things that happened to me throughout my college experience. During my one-on-one meetings with him, I was able to make huge transformations in my life that once seemed unchangeable. From working out family differences and dealing with closure, to finding my voice, I've learned to better my interpersonal relationships in every aspect. Mr. Armiento has helped me grow mentally and spiritually by giving me the tools of meditation and visualization which made a tremendous impact on my life. In the sport of track and field, which to me is 90% mental, focus is vital and not always the easiest thing to do. But with the knowledge of meditation and visualization it comes easy. Meditation has enhanced my spirituality and the process of visualization has given me the collegiate career that I literally dreamt of.

The growth that I've endured within the two years of knowing Mr. Armiento is unbelievable. I am a living testament of Mr. Armiento's work and the experience that I've had with him is one that I would recommend to anyone who wants a better life. I just wanted to say thank you for all your love and support, all your help and just being so wonderful to me!

I don't know what the end result would have been without you but I know I'm a whole better person because I know you. I end my season with no regrets and I am so grateful to God for the honor of being an Olympian. Thank you and love you."

Phobay Kutu-Akoi, 2012 Olympian, London – Liberia's 100m Dash Record Holder

"Our coaching staff considers Mark Armiento an invaluable resource for not only our players but for our support and guidance in many major decisions that we make as a staff. Mark has helped our team in a multitude of areas. We have seen tremendous personal and performance growth in all of our players who have sought his counseling. As a coaching staff, we seek out his expertise on group management throughout the year. The sessions he leads that force our team to work as a high functioning group teach our players skills in communicating and listening effectively. Mark is an instrumental piece in achieving our aim of empowering the young women in our program to great success on and off the field".

Ian Stone, Head Coach St. John's University Women's Soccer

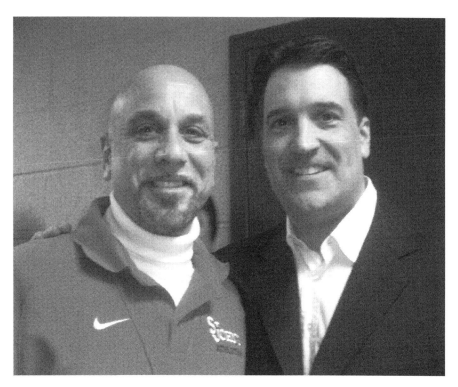

"I've worked with Mark for almost 6 years now both individually and in group/team work. His ability to immerse himself in the energies of others is very unique and special. I feel both pride and deep gratitude that the universe has placed Mark in my journey and would encourage anyone to invite Mark into their journey as a very special gift/opportunity. Working with Mark, both inside and outside athletics, I have discovered extremely powerful tools inside myself that I didn't even know existed. I have come to connect with myself in ways that I didn't even know were possible! Whether I was running to Mark's office in between classes or soccer practice for in-person sessions or whether we have our sessions via skype from South America to North, it continues to be a life-giving process of growth, connection, and discoveries that I simply can't describe via typing. It's just not that "black and white" and in fact continues to exude a myriad of brightness that surpasses all color charts."

Jess Simonetti, former St. Johns University Women's Soccer.
Ph.D candidate, Palo Alto University

"After only two meetings with Mark, my performance felt like it made a 180 degree turn around. After struggling for quite a while with my confidence and drive, I decided to make the initiative to get some help. Never having been the type to ask for help, making this initiative was a new experience and I had my doubts. Mark has a great inviting personality and his friendliness put me at ease, especially when it was such a novice experience. In the initial hour I had spent, I learned more about myself, and about the interrelations that take place in my life, than I had ever expected. I'd communicate with Mark between meetings to "stay on track". The night before a competition I had talked to Mark to help with some emotions that had been interfering with my performance. The next day, I had felt like a completely different person. I was confident, strong, determines and "in the zone". I competed at my absolute peak; I haven't felt that amazing in a while. I can't thank Mark enough for enlightening and guiding me through all the stresses of life. Not only has his guidance helped my performance, but also my everyday life. Mark is phenomenal, and I would recommend him to all my fellow student athletes!"

Alexandra Tannous – Lebanese National Fencing Team,

"On a personal level, working with Mark has given me access to tools, such as meditation techniques, to continue on my path to self-awareness. I have gained a sense of peace in all aspects of my life and have uncovered new depths of creative energies. This has directly had a positive impact on my interactions with others as well, particularly as a coach and teacher. I am also proud to have been a part of Mark's work with the St. John's women's soccer program. I am very grateful for the time he spends sharing tools, such as goal setting and communication skills, with young women to contribute to their academic, athletic and personal success."

Michele Canning, NYU Head Women's Soccer Coach / Former Women's Soccer Coach at St. John's University

"Mark Armiento was the Sports Psychologist for the student-athletes at St. John's University. I was someone who never saw a psychologist for any therapy on or off the field, and was hesitant about doing so, but I finally walked into his office in my senior year of college. I felt like I was under heavy emotional and physical stress when I came in for my first session and Mr. Armiento far surpassed any expectations I had of a counselor. As a third party to both my personal and sports related situations, he truly helped me cope and understand myself better in order to deal with these stressful and emotional situations that I usually could never speak to anyone about. I can honestly say he helped me through a very tough time in my life and saw me through it until I felt better. I would recommend Mr. Armiento to anybody over and over again." Top Qualities: Great Results, Good Value, High Integrity

Nakita Austin, 2012 Outstanding Athlete of the Year, Division I Tennis

"I have witnessed Mark's work and am most impressed at his ability to make people feel comfortable and valid in their beliefs. He challenges individuals to create a healthy balance in life in order to achieve an optimum lifestyle. Professionally, he has successfully worked with many of my student-athletes. He is always available and accommodating. Most recently he spoke to an athlete via telephone on a Saturday night prior to a game on Sunday and she had one of her stronger performances in weeks. He is very thorough in his work."

Amy Kvilhaug, Head Softball Coach at St. John's University

"Mark, You are the best and I appreciate all your help with Phobay (2012 Olympian) and all the others you have helped. Phobay has come full circle and it is has been an incredible journey and a great St. John's story. Mark, Thanks again for all your great work with Phobay. Seeing her march in the opening ceremonies watching her compete in front of 80,000 people in the Olympic stadium against the top sprinters on the planet really was remarkable and I know you had a great part in getting her there. From the Liberia to Maryland to the hallway in Carnesecca in Queens to the Olympic Stadium in London is some journey and one you had a helping hand in. I truly appreciate it, thank you for all your great effort, and ask that you keep up the good work."

Jim Hurt, Head Track & Field Coach at St. John's University

"Mark has been an outstanding resource to our baseball program. He has been there for several of our players. On a personal note, I have attended several of Mark's Life Balance workshops. I have found them to be very informative and helpful. I have incorporated many of Mark's life balance suggestions. His presentation encourages interaction and is extremely thought provoking."

Ed Blankmeyer, Head Baseball Coach at St. John's University

"Mark's workshops are very useful to our organization as he

understands our department and adapts his expertise to ensure every participant receives quality, relevant content. He is passionate about his life's vocation, and that comes across throughout the presentation and in his ability to connect with everyone in the room! His workshops remind me to stay attentive to the goals that really matter in my life while assisting me to develop personal tools to ensure that I actually achieve the goals I set out to accomplish. It has been a pleasure to work with Mark throughout my career at St. John's as the head women's volleyball coach. He is a critical component of our three-time Big East Champion team!"

Joanne Persico, Head Volleyball Coach at St. John's University

"Mark is of great assistance in developing our student-athletes not only on the playing field but in their aspirations to achieve academically, socially and in the community. He is a great "coach" for our student athletes"

Chris Monasch, Athletic Director at St. John's University, New York

"Mark, I wanted to let you know how grateful I am to you and for everything you've taught me. There have been times recently, when I have been in a new situation and have felt completely at peace and prepared to handle new challenges-I have never before felt this confidence! What you have taught me has shaped who I am -I owe you so much and I hope you know how grateful I am to have been able to learn from you over the past few years."

Nicole Canning PT, DPT, St. John's 2011 graduate – Women's Soccer athlete

"Mark's emphasis on balance is an important lesson for optimal athletic performance. Student-athletes have many competing stresses in their lives-academically, athletically, socially and emotionally.

Through Mark's work, he teaches students the importance of identifying these situations while providing them the tools to develop appropriate strategies to effectively manage all aspects of their lives"

Patrick Elliot, Director of Athletics at Binghamton University, New York

"Mark is deeply committed to helping people grow personally and spiritually. With his formidable skills and creativity his greatest gift is the personal presence and his commitment to accompanying people in their times of need. He is a blessing to all he serves"

Fr. James Maher, President, Niagara University

"It has been 20 years since Mark Armiento first invited me to "awaken to the dance of life" I was an RN with 25 years of nursing experience now working in an adolescent drug treatment program and he was my supervisor. In that capacity he empowered me to attain the life skills tools by which to evolve from a somewhat codependent human doing into the spiritual being having a human experience that I am today. Mark found a way to subtly become my life coach before this term was ever defined. Every project I undertook with his guidance simply could not fail. Consequently, through efficient time management, interpersonal and communication skills, stress management, leadership skills trainings and personal self-challenge he provided, I have achieved success in my Nursing Career beyond my imagination. Mark is a skilled clinician and a visionary who sees clearly the self-limiting issues others impose on themselves and you have the unique ability to provide the guidance needed to transcend and achieve."

Joan M. Lohnes RN, LMHC

"When I was hired as Fort Lauderdale's City Manager many years ago, I reached out for Mark's help in rebuilding the City's management team so we could better address a government in organizational meltdown. I needed a management team that could quickly and effectively address a financial crisis that had left the City with no reserves, a major insurance deficit, reductions in services, downgraded bond ratings, an employee exodus, and general public dissatisfaction. I had worked with Mark before and I knew how effective he was at getting a group of people to excel individually and collectively. Mark's team building and peak performance strategies produced amazing results and our team started winning games in a big way. In a very short period of time, we were able to restore the City's financial health and improve City services. Today, the City's financial position is stronger than it has been in the City's history, with a record high fund balance, a $10 million insurance surplus, an upgraded bond rating that ranks among the best of Florida's largest cities, and property taxes and fees that rank among the lowest of Florida's largest cities. Our 'peak performance' team has also produced significant results on quality of life issues. Since 2006, Fort Lauderdale has enjoyed its lowest crime rate in over 30 years. Property crimes reached their lowest levels in over 30 years. The streets and sidewalks are cleaner, the medians are better maintained, and code violations are resolved more quickly.

As a manager of an organization of 2,600 employees with two decades of government experience, I can honestly say that Mark Armiento is the best I have ever seen at inspiring greatness in government employees."

Mr. George Gretsas, Esq. City Manager: 2004 to 2010, City of Fort Lauderdale Current Homestead, Fla. City Manager

"Our CEO brought Mark in to work with our management team. Few expected any real improvement to our performance; none expected the positive transformation that our team underwent. Accountability and ownership increased, and department heads who wouldn't talk to one another began working together synergistically. Personally, working with Mark has had a remarkably positive impact. The tools he has given me have allowed me to achieve previously impossible results, including rising to COO of my organization."

Ted Lawson, Former Assistant City Manager,
Fort Lauderdale, FL

Anthony's Story

When you are comfortable in your own skin you can achieve anything. Unfortunately at the age of 18, I cared about others way more than myself. My whole life I didn't really care what others thought of me until my success on the baseball field became public. As a freshman going into St. Johns my life took a detour. I was worrying about things I could not control, and others perceptions of myself rather than what I knew to be true. I lost friends, my high school girlfriend, and my inner confidence. Being stripped of the things I loved most felt like a stab in the back from the universe. At the time I felt betrayed by my life and everything I worked so hard for.

I truly thought I would be ordinary and plain like a lot of people who just live to exist. This fear grew, and grew, and grew. The fear of being average broke my heart, and left me alone in my comfort zone. Knowing myself I knew something wasn't right. Little did I know I was going to meet one of the most amazing, caring, and loving individual in my life at the start of my freshman year. I reached out to Mark Armiento after I attended one of his presentations during freshman orientation. While my ego was telling me I was too good to get help from someone, something louder and more persistent encouraged me to do differently.

Immediately after meeting with him I felt accepted. The way he spoke had me hooked. I wanted to learn everything this man had to teach. But as I would come to realize great things take time. Every week of my freshman year I would meet with Mark for a casual conversation about life. I can honestly say that in the 30 minutes we talked each week I learned more from Mark then I had from any teacher or coach who has every taught me. His way of breaking down the limitations I held inside of myself left me confused with myself and intrigued at the same time. After a while I began to realize I found something special.

The rest of my freshman year went by quick, and I was feeling better. Not where I wanted to be but better. At the beginning of my sophomore year Mark taught me TM, or more commonly known as Transcendental Meditation. This technique took a lot of preparation, but later on would benefit me more than any single practice in my life. Learning to listen to my mind, and separate my ego from my intuition helped me transform negativity into positivity. Mark gave me examples of using that driving force I found inside of myself as a tool to connect with something deeper inside that couldn't quite come out. It was scared and unprepared to be revealed to the people around it. I wish I wouldn't have been in such a rush to figure out everything he was teaching me, but eventually this would all make sense.

As my sophomore year began, I was coming off a good summer season and some fun experiences. Still there was something eating away at me. My fears of not being good enough took over. It was becoming the script of my life. Scared I wasn't good enough, not like the others, and average. Every time my light would shine I would dim it down to make others comfortable. I continued my conversations with Mark and began to really understand some key things. We talked about things that I was experiencing that not many people could relate to.

Eager to enjoy my second year of college I was in rush to get to the season. I did well during the fall, but I knew deep down I was better than I was performing. At the beginning of my spring sophomore season I really hit a wall. Another injury came up, and I was forced to redshirt. Down in the dumps again, I chose to leave St. John's

University due to some issues that had arose over time with my team and the coaching staff. My heart wasn't fully into the program that I had once loved so much. With no school to attend the next year, and 6 months of rehab I was back at square one. Still I pushed through and Mark was there to help me the whole time.

Some personal issues came up in early June and I really hit rock bottom. While working three Jobs all summer, training for baseball, taking care of my family, and feeling worse than I ever had I reached out to Mark again! I was broke and angry. I sat and wondered why this was all happening to me and my family. A quick talk with Mark help put things in perspective. So instead of being a product of my environment, I chose to create an environment. This time I knew there was no other option but to push through. This period of adversity changed my life. I went from victim, to champion. I left old habits and developed new productive ones. After two years I was finally starting to feel like myself again in a time of true turmoil. Bad news after bad news, I knew I wasn't going to live like this anymore.

I was in my hometown and had had the opportunity to get in touch with my roots and where I came from. I went back to a time where I was driven from within. Not by things going on around me. I became humbled again from helping my family and others. Feeling blessed and grateful I took it upon myself to get myself and my family to better place. After conversations with Mark during this time, my self-awareness grew thanks to his insights about Life Balance. He assured me that God gives his greatest challenges to his strongest warriors. And after a long period of struggle my phone rang one late October night. It was my old teammate who is now a professional baseball player for the Houston Astros. He told me about a school down in Oklahoma and recommended me to the coach since I had nowhere to go to school. Three days later I was on a plane to Oklahoma City with my vivid dream of becoming a Major League Baseball Player. I felt so alive and determined to become the person I knew I was.

I stayed in contact with Mark throughout my journey. One of Marks specific teachings about comfort zones that he had taught me my freshman year finally made sense. You see the genius behind him is that he guides you away from the wrong and towards the right choices without letting fear be the deciding factor in your decisions. He will never tell you exactly what to do unless he absolutely feels he has to intervene and give you a wake you up call. But Mark knew I got my wakeup call from something greater.

"There are two kinds of teachers: the kind that fill you with so much quail shot that you can't move, and the kind that just give you a little prod behind and you jump to the skies" - Robert Frost

I arrived not knowing one person, and with 63 dollars to my name, but I didn't care. I had baseball, and a team to play for. I was honored to be a student athlete again. Baseball began to become fun instead of a job, and I immediately clicked with my teammates and coaches. Mark always recommended getting away from everything and finding myself on my own. Now I am in the middle of my season and have never been so happy in my entire life. I feel blessed to see how far I've come. Today, I can hold my head high with confidence and say I am the man I want my son to be. The person I want my parents to be proud of. The teammate you go to for advice. The guy who wants to help people just to make someone else's day better because I know how it feels to be on the other side.

Pain and failure made me who I am today. It's not all the times I've won, but the times I've lost that I learned from the most. And the funny part about it all is that my fears have become the best source of motivation I've ever had. I fear staying the same, and not progressing. Fear lets me enjoy the challenges I face today. Knowing I will learn from loss instead of feeling like a victim, I chose to win or learn no matter what. I chose to live a life behind the steering wheel instead of in the passenger seat. I've learned to love the distractions because they remind me of how focused I am. I have an inner peace that no one can shake. My faith in God, and trust in myself has led me to become the leader that I am today.

Now as of March 26, 2015 I have offers from Division 1 colleges, and the opportunity to be drafted at the end of the 2015 season. And truthfully the one person who I have to thank for all the help they have given me throughout this two year detour is Mark Armiento. From sharing his own experiences I've learned to forgive myself for things I've done in the past. Most importantly Mark has helped me use my fear as a gift. I have learned to love my fear. I love when my mind says I can't do something because it makes me work that much harder to prove my fears wrong. I want to stand for something greater than myself. I want to stand for the idea that you can accomplish your dreams no matter what anyone tells you. I've had people doubting me my whole life just because I am talented at what I do. Mark helped me realize that the only person who can stop you is you. Not a critic, or an enemy. You and what you do each and every day are the only things in control of your future. He's given me tips to control my mind, body, emotions, relationships, inner spirit and trade my need for attention for respect. Best of all, I am fortunate enough to have known who I am and what I've wanted to do from a very young age. For that I thank God and will not let his gift to me go to waste.

There's a certain flow that the universe operates in. If you can catch that wave and ride it you can do anything you want. Never believe that something is too good to be true. All you need to know is who you are what you want to do. Once you figure that out than you must sacrifice everything that is not necessary. Your struggles will manifest into things bigger then you can imagine if you truly work for it. I promise you that if you picture something in your mind and really visualize it you can do it. Through meditation you can relax and let the answers come to you instead of worrying about the answers you seek. The solutions will come if you let them. Today I am obsessively dedicated to being the best that I can be. Develop a routine and truly believe there's nothing that can stop you. Great things take time.

If I could go back to the 18 year old me I would tell him to relax and enjoy the ride. Also don't try to be anything you're not. But yet again everything I'm not made me everything I am. I would also say don't be in such a rush to get anywhere and truly enjoy each moment that life gives you because once it is gone, it is gone forever.

Mark Armiento has given me a second chance to enjoy the wave-Another opportunity to take control over my life. I had nothing to offer Mark at all. A blessing in disguise, he is one of the most sincere individuals I have ever met. Not many people can say they dedicate themselves to bettering the lives of others. And if they do, I can assure you there is just something so special about the way this man can make you feel. Not one time did I feel worse leaving him then I did arriving. He will believe in you even if you don't. So from the bottom of my heart I want to say thank him for everything. And especially for helping me love myself and my life. I now accept things the way they are, and have the courage to change them thanks to Mark Armiento and his Life Balance Advantage.

God Bless

Anthony Rosati

REFERENCES

Chapter 1

Life Quotes, http://www.brainyquote.com/quotes/topics/topic_life.html

Why Is Spirituality Important? http://www.takingcharge.csh.umn.edu/ enhance-your-wellbeing/purpose/spirituality/why-spirituality-important

Why is Spirituality Important? — The Importance of Spirituality, http:// lifeandself.com/why-is-spirituality-important-the-importance-of- spirituality/

Juline, Kathy, *Awakening Your Life's Purposes,* http://www.eckharttolle. com/article/Awakening-Your-Spiritual-Lifes-Purpose

Carey, Benedict, *Who's Minding The Mind?* http://www.nytimes. com/2007/07/31/health/psychology/31subl.html?pagewanted=all&_r=0

Kurus, Mary, *How Do We View Health Today,* http://www.mkprojects. com/fa_PEMHealth.htm

Subconscious Mind And Its Impact On Our Behavior, http://www. tonyfahkry.com/subconscious-mind-and-its-impact-on-our-behaviour/

Ria, Natalia, *Signs And Symptoms Of Spiritual Awakening,* http://in5d. com/signs-and-symptoms-of-a-spiritual-awakening/

Annarita, *Symptoms Of Spiritual Awakening,* http://www.sunfell.com/ symptoms.htm

Chapter 2

Campbell, Joseph, *Quotes,* http://www.brainyquote.com/quotes/ quotes/j/josephcamp386014.html

Listening To Your Guiding Whispers, http://healing.about.com/od/ selfpower/a/wisdom_voice.htm

Juntilla, Henri, *How To Hear Your Inner Wisdom When Making Tough Choices,* http://tinybuddha.com/blog/hear-inner-wisdom-making-tough-choices/

Leuthold, Scott, *Understanding The Awakening Process,* http://www. tokenrock.com/articles/understanding-the-awakening-process-68.html

Unconsciously Unaware To Subconsciously Aware, http://www. alephsynergy.com/processes-awareness/Unconsciously-to-Subconsciously-aware.html

Conscious And Competence, http://changingminds.org/explanations/ learning/consciousness_competence.htm

The Conscious Competence Ladder, http://www.mindtools.com/pages/ article/newISS_96.htm

Four Levels Of Self-Awareness And Self-Empowerment, http://www.voice-dialogue-inner-self-awareness.com/Four%20Levels81.html

Chapter 3

Self-Awareness Quotes, http://www.brainyquote.com/quotes/keywords/ self-awareness.html

Klosowski, Thorin, *The Importance Of Self-Awareness, And How To Become More Self Aware,* http://lifehacker.com/the-importance-of-self-awareness-and-how-to-become-mor-1624744518

Goldstein, Elisha, Ph.D, *The Neuroscience Of Resistance And How To Overcome It,* http://blogs.psychcentral.com/mindfulness/2014/09/the-neuroscience-of-resistance-and-how-to-overcome-it/

Simon, George, Dr, *Impulsive Thinking, Impulsive Actions, Dire Consequences,* http://counsellingresource.com/features/2008/12/29/ impulsive-thinking/

Sircus, Dr, *The Ego As The Root Of Conflict,* http://drsircus.com/ personal/the-ego-as-the-root-of-conflict

Strategies To Overcome Ego, http://humanscience.wikia.com/wiki/ Strategies_to_overcome_ego

Seven Primary Obstacles To Self Awareness, http://gaiancorps.com/study/psychology-mind/fourth-way/the-basics/item/29-seven-primary-obstacles-to-self-awareness

Self-Awareness And Personal Responsibility, http://www.sosoft.com/blog/2011/06/06/self-awareness-and-personal-responsibility/

Accepting Personal/Self Responsibility, http://www.theawarenessparty.com/links-and-resources/articles/scientific/spontaneous-evolution/accepting-personal-self-responsibility/

Maisel, Eric, Dr, *Tips For Overcoming Internal Barriers To Success,* http://lifepluswork.com/tips-for-overcoming-internal-barriers-to-success/

McLeod, Saul, *Self-Concept,* http://www.simplypsychology.org/self-concept.html

Chapter 4

Joseph Campbell Quotes, http://www.brainyquote.com/quotes/authors/j/joseph_campbell.html

Realization For Change, http://mymeditativemoments.com/realization-for-change/

The Effects Of Stress On The Body, http://www.healthline.com/health/stress/effects-on-body

Self-Awareness – The Key To Breaking Bad Habits, http://www.mind-awakening-techniques.com/self-awareness-bad-habits.php

Hiskey, Daven, *Humans Have A lot More Than Five Senses,* http://www.todayifoundout.com/index.php/2010/07/humans-have-a-lot-more-than-five-senses/

Diener, Ed, Lucas, Richard E, Oishi, Shigehiro, *Subjective Well-Being,* http://greatergood.berkeley.edu/images/application_uploads/Diener-Subjective_Well-Being.pdf

Sasson, Remez, *Emotional Detachment For A Better Life,* http://www.successconsciousness.com/books/emotional-detachment-for-better-life.html

Corbin, Kate, *The Magic Of Focus,* http://www.selfgrowth.com/articles/the-magic-of-focus

Babauta, Leo, *The Magical Power Of Focus*, http://zenhabits.net/the-magical-power-of-focus/

Tanjeloff, Jasmin, *How To Create A Balanced Life: 9 Tips To Feel Calm And Grounded*, http://tinybuddha.com/blog/9-tips-to-create-a-balanced-life/

Moss Kantor, Rosabeth, *Ten Reasons People Resist Change*, https://hbr.org/2012/09/ten-reasons-people-resist-chang.html

Chapter 5

Thought Quotes, http://www.brainyquote.com/quotes/keywords/thoughts.html

Conwell, Russell, H, *Acres Of Diamonds: Our Everyday Opportunities*, http://www.gutenberg.org/files/368/368-h/368-h.htm

de Bruin, Dirk, *Simplify Your Life By Eliminating These 7 Problems*, http://tinybuddha.com/blog/simplify-your-life-by-eliminating-these-7-problems/

Self-Healing Process, http://www.spiritual-healing-for-you.com/self-healing-process.html

Stress: How To Cope Better With Life's Challenges, http://familydoctor.org/familydoctor/en/prevention-wellness/emotional-wellbeing/mental-health/stress-how-to-cope-better-with-lifes-challenges.html

Kehoe, John, *Eliminating Negative Thinking*, http://www.learnmindpower.com/using_mindpower/eliminating_negative_thinking/

Woods, Ron, *"Energy Management" Leads To Good Health, Positive Outlook*, http://www.humankinetics.com/excerpts/excerpts/energy-management-leads-to-good-health-positive-outlook

Schwartz, Tony, McCarthy, Catherine, *Manage Your Energy, Not Your Time*, https://hbr.org/2007/10/manage-your-energy-not-your-time

Chapter 6

Thought Quotes, http://www.brainyquote.com/quotes/keywords/thoughts.html

Ellis, Theo, J, *Why Smart People Commit To Self Improvement Everyday*, http://justbereal.co.uk/why-smart-people-commit-to-self-improvement-everyday/

Cole, Terri, *How To Become The Observer And Liberate Yourself,* http://www.positivelypositive.com/2014/03/14/how-to-become-the-observer-and-liberate-yourself/

Observing Yourself, http://www.lessons4living.com/observing_yourself.htm

Formica, Michael, J, *5 Steps For Being Present,* https://www.psychologytoday.com/blog/enlightened-living/201106/5-steps-being-present

Kelley, Jean, *Forget Time management... Are You Managing Your Energy?* http://www.affluentmagazine.com/articles/article/664

Rose, Angelica, *Awakening The Inner Spirit,* http://www.awakening360.com/article/awakening-the-inner-spirit-angelica_rose#sthash.Eo6Jhgi6.dpbs

Radwan, M, Farouk, MSc, *How To Use The Weapon Of Attention To Attract People To You,* http://www.2knowmyself.com/attention_and_attracting_people_to_you

How Influence Works, http://www.theelementsofpower.com/index.cfm/how-influence-works/

Deepak Chopra: How To Recognize Life's Abundance, http://www.oprah.com/spirit/Deepak-Chopra-How-to-Feel-More-Fulfilled

Byers, Jeanine, *How To Uncover Your Life Purpose Even If You Have No Idea!* http://www.trans4mind.com/counterpoint/index-life-purpose/byers.shtml

Chapter 7

Balance Quotes, http://www.brainyquote.com/quotes/keywords/balance.html

Living a Balanced Life in an Unbalanced World, http://advancedlifeskills.com/blog/seeking-balance-in-an-unbalanced-world/

Farbota, Kim, *5 Steps To Maximize Efficiency By Managing Your Energy, Not Your Time,* http://www.huffingtonpost.com/kim-farbota/success-and-motivation_b_5367183.html

Vhernoff, Marc, *19 Toxic Habits That Drain Your Energy,* http://www.marcandangel.com/2014/08/24/10-toxic-habits-that-drain-your-energy/

A Balanced Life – Can You Really Have It All? http://www.mommd.com/canyouhaveitall.shtml

Core, Andy, *The Importance Of Work-Life Balance For Increased Workplace Productivity,* http://andycore.com/importance-work-life-balance-higher-productivity-workplace/

Wang, Bo, *The Role Of Direct-To-Consumer Pharmaceutical Advertising In Patient Consumerism,* http://journalofethics.ama-assn.org/2013/11/pfor1-1311.html

Energy Balance, http://apjcn.nhri.org.tw/server/info/books-phds/books/foodfacts/html/maintext/main5a.html

Emotionally Centered: Passion Power & Rationalization Ruin, http://www.themichaelteaching.com/sessions/no-fault-communication/passions-rationalizations/

Chapter 8

Balance Quotes, http://www.brainyquote.com/quotes/keywords/balance.html

Widrich, Leo, *The Four Elements Of Physical Energy And How To Master Them,* https://blog.bufferapp.com/the-4-elements-of-physical-energy-on-how-to-master-them

Mind/Body Connection: How Your Emotions Affect Your Health, http://familydoctor.org/familydoctor/en/prevention-wellness/emotional-wellbeing/mental-health/mind-body-connection-how-your-emotions-affect-your-health.html

Emotional Wellness, http://wellness.ucr.edu/emotional_wellness.html

Winch, Guy, *5 Habits That Will Improve Your Emotional Wellness,* http://www.huffingtonpost.com/guy-winch-phd/emotional-wellness-tips_b_3809750.html

Clear, James, *The Science Of Developing Mental Toughness In Your Health, Work, And Life,* http://jamesclear.com/mental-toughness

Morin, Amy, *5 Powerful Exercises To Increase Your Mental Strength,* http://www.forbes.com/sites/groupthink/2013/12/03/5-powerful-exercises-to-increase-your-mental-strength/

Increase Your Mental Clarity In Just 15 Minutes, http://personalexcellence.co/blog/increase-your-mental-clarity-in-just-15-minutes/

Su, Tina, *How To Organize Mental Clutter*, http://thinksimplenow.com/productivity/how-to-organize-mental-clutter/

Gemma, Will, *List Of Interpersonal Skills: 10 Must-Have Attributes,* https://blog.udemy.com/list-of-interpersonal-skills/

Social Wellness – What Social Wellness Is, https://socialwellness.wordpress.com/what-social-wellness-is/

Bizjak, Paul, *The Importance Of Social Wellness,* http://movetowardwellness.com/what-is-wellness/social-wellness

Chapter 9

Balance, http://www.ramaquotes.com/html/balance.html

Spiritual Wellness, http://wellness.ucr.edu/spiritual_wellness.html

Spiritual Longing And The Path Of Forgiveness, http://www.worldblessings.com/spiritual-longing.html

Krishnananda, Swami, Living A Spiritual Life, http://www.swami-krishnananda.org/spiritual.life/spiritual_09.html

Albrecht, Karl, The (Only) Seven Spiritual Principles We Need To Succeed, https://www.psychologytoday.com/blog/brainsnacks/201301/the-only-seven-spiritual-principles-we-need-succeed

Codorniu, Vanessa, Got Spirit? Five Simple Ways To Feel Spiritually Connected NOW, http://www.selfgrowth.com/articles/got-spirit-five-simple-ways-to-feel-spiritually-connected-now

Chapter 10

Health Quotes, http://www.brainyquote.com/quotes/topics/topic_health.html

The Signs And Symptoms Of A Nervous Breakdown You Should Not Ignore, http://www.professional-counselling.com/nervousbreakdown_

panic_attack.html#.VQWKX_mUepc

The Science Of Raw Food, http://www.rawfoodlife.com/#axzz3USgVDWri

Lang, Steven, Live Foods, https://experiencelife.com/article/live-foods/

Widrick, Leo, What Happens To Our Brains When We Exercise And How It Makes Us Happier, https://blog.bufferapp.com/why-exercising-makes-us-happier

Why Is Exercise Important? http://www.healthdiscovery.net/articles/exercise_importa.htm

Relaxation Techniques: Try These Steps To Reduce Stress, http://www.mayoclinic.org/healthy-living/stress-management/in-depth/relaxation-technique/art-20045368

Healthy Eating Strategies, http://life.familyeducation.com/foods/nutrition-and-diet/44296.html

Pear, Robert, Psychiatric Drug Overuse Is Cited By Federal Study, http://www.nytimes.com/2015/03/02/us/psychiatric-drug-overuse-is-cited-by-federal-study.html?_r=0

West, Corinna, What We Can Do About The Overuse Of Psychiatric Drugs, http://corinnawest.com/what-we-can-do-about-the-overuse-of-psychiatric-medications/

Simonds, Seth, Sleep Hack: A Simple Strategy For Better Rest In Less Time, http://www.lifehack.org/articles/lifehack/sleep-hack-a-simple-strategy-for-better-rest-in-less-time.html

Chapter 11

Emotions Quotes, http://www.brainyquote.com/quotes/keywords/emotions.html

Biancalana, Roy**,** *What To Do When You're An Emotional Wreck.* http://coachingwithroy.com/what-to-do-when-youre-an-emotional-wreck/

Stephenson, Janet, Louise, *Choosing NOT To Be An Emotional Wreck,* http://www.butterfly-maiden.com/personal-development/emotional-wreck

Razzaque, Russell, *The Universal Value Of Emotional Intelligence,* https://

www.psychologytoday.com/blog/political-intelligence/201206/the-universal-value-emotional-intelligence

Overcoming F.E.A.R.: False Evidence Appearing Real, http://www.awaken.com/2013/01/overcoming-f-e-a-r-false-evidence-appearing-real/

5 Ways Keeping A Journal Can Help You De-Stress, http://www.huffingtonpost.com/2013/02/13/5-ways-keeping-a-journal-_n_2671735.html

Mayer, John, D, Geher, Glenn, *Emotional Intelligence And The Identification Of Emotion,* http://www.unh.edu/emotional_intelligence/EI%20Assets/Reprints...EI%20Proper/EI1996MayerGeher.pdf

Unconscious Ideas And Emotions, http://www.psychologistworld.com/emotion/emotion_5.php

Parry, Greer, *Living Right Now: You Are Not Your Thoughts And Feelings,* http://tinybuddha.com/blog/living-right-now-you-are-not-your-thoughts-and-feelings/

Kotsos, Tania, *Rise Above Your Emotions – Be The Witness Not The Puppet,* http://www.mind-your-reality.com/above_your_emotions.html

Transcending Our Reactive Emotions, http://www.innerfrontier.org/InnerWork/Archive/2014/20141006_Reactive_Emotions.htm

Chapter 12

Mentality Quotes, http://www.brainyquote.com/quotes/keywords/mentality.html

Bijou, Jude, *Six Simple Steps To Cure Confusion,* http://attitudereconstruction.com/2013/10/six-simple-steps-to-cure-confusion/

Decision Making And Indecisiveness Tendencies In Our Nature, http://www.charminghealth.com/applicability/decision-making.htm

Self-Esteem That's Based On External Sources Has Mental Health Consequences, Study Says, http://www.apa.org/monitor/dec02/selfesteem.aspx

Sheridan, Tonya, *The Forgotten Trait Of Self-Respect,* http://www.mindbodygreen.com/0-2800/The-Forgotten-Trait-of-SelfRespect.html

Fern, Ashley, *Why You Need To Learn From Your Mistakes*, http://elitedaily.com/life/why-you-need-to-learn-from-your-mistakes/

Mind Power – How To Break Free Of Limiting Beliefs, http://www.wellbeingalignment.com/mind-power.html

Law Of Attraction – The Power Of Beliefs, http://www.mind-sets.com/html/law_of_attraction/the_power_of_beliefs.htm

Golden Rules Of Goal Setting, http://www.mindtools.com/pages/article/newHTE_90.htm

Sasson, Remez, *How To Be Optimistic*, http://www.successconsciousness.com/how-to-be-optimistic.htm

Invoking Resourceful States, http://voice2vision.net/invoking-resourceful-states/

Klosowski, Thorin, *How Your Expectations Mess With Your View Of The Present*, http://lifehacker.com/how-your-expectations-mess-with-your-view-of-the-presen-1685353419

Chapter 13

Interpersonal Quotes, http://www.brainyquote.com/quotes/keywords/interpersonal.html

Richards, Thomas, A, *What Is It Like To Live With Social Anxiety?* https://socialanxietyinstitute.org/living-with-social-anxiety

Wert, Ken, *12 Ways To Forgive Your Parents For Doing Such A Crummy Job Of Raising You,* http://www.stevenaitchison.co.uk/blog/12-ways-to-forgive-your-parents/

Nguyen, Veronica, *Learning To Forgive Our Imperfect Parents For Their Mistakes,* http://tinybuddha.com/blog/learning-to-forgive-our-imperfect-parents-for-their-mistakes/

Bowlin, Yvette, *5 Signs You're In A Toxic Relationship,* http://tinybuddha.com/blog/5-signs-youre-in-a-toxic-relationship/

Borchard, Therese, J, *You Deplete Me: 10 Steps To End A Toxic Relationship,* http://psychcentral.com/blog/archives/2010/03/15/you-deplete-me-10-steps-to-end-a-toxic-relationship/

Use Body Language To Build Rapport, http://www.businessweek.com/smallbiz/tips/archives/2010/11/use_body_language_to_build_rapport.html

Being Consciously Aware Of Your Speech, http://lightworkers.org/channeling/193676/being-consciously-aware-your-speech

Chapter 14

Spirituality Quotes, http://www.brainyquote.com/quotes/keywords/spirituality.html

Klinsky, Leslee, J, *Aligning With Your Higher Self,* http://healing.about.com/od/higherself/a/alignhigherself.htm

Rose, Phil, Fox, *What Works: Spiritual Recovery,* http://bustedhalo.com/features/what-works-6-spiritual-recovery

Brussat, Frederic, Brussat, Mary Ann, *Harvesting Memories – Reaping The Blessings And Lessons Of The Past,* http://www.spiritualityandpractice.com/practices/features.php?id=17004

St. Claire, Claudia, *21 Essential Tricks For Achieving Spiritual Balance In The Midst Of Chaos,* http://thoughtcatalog.com/claudia-st-clair/2014/02/21-essential-tricks-for-achieving-spiritual-balance-in-the-midst-of-chaos/

Spiritual Enlightening – Reception Of The Divine Energy, http://www.trivedieffect.com/spiritual-enlightening-reception-of-the-divine-energy

ABOUT THE AUTHOR

Mark's quest: To teach self-healing through the Life Balance Advantage so that they can own the happiness they deserve and know they are blessed

For over 30 years, Mark has been providing clinical, consultation, and training services for professionals in the areas of personal development, alcohol and substance abuse, sports performance, organizational management, and general health and wellness. He holds New York State licenses in Marriage & Family Therapy and in Mental Health Counseling. A clinical member of the American Association of Marriage and Family Therapists (AAMFT), he holds a New York State Credential in Alcohol and Drug Counseling (CASAC) as well as advanced certificates in Neuro Linguistic Programming (NLP), Hypnosis, Auricular Acupuncture, Trauma Reduction (EMDR) Transcendental Meditation (TM), and Reiki. Mark is the former Vice President of a large N.Y. non-profit company whose mission is to empower individuals, families, and communities to make choices that will enable them to experience a responsible life free from alcohol and drug abuse. He has designed and directed multiple, award winning addictions education institutes. Mark has delivered organizational management consulting for various cities, such as Ft. Lauderdale and Homestead, Florida. He has been a sport psychology consultant for the Liberian International Athletics Foundation for the 2012 and 2016 Olympics and is currently a sports psychology and counseling consultant for New York universities.

Made in the USA
Middletown, DE
25 June 2020